# ARTHUR
# CONAN
# DOYLE

# ARTHUR CONAN DOYLE

## THE MAN BEHIND SHERLOCK HOLMES

### ANDREW NORMAN

*To my dear wife, Rachel*

First published 2007
This edition published 2009

The History Press
The Mill, Brimscombe Port
Stroud, Gloucestershire, GL5 2QG
www.thehistorypress.co.uk

British Library Cataloguing in Publication Data.
A catalogue record for this book is available from the British Library.

ISBN 978 0 7524 5275 3

Typesetting and origination by The History Press
Printed in Great Britain

# Contents

# Acknowledgements

Office of the Chief Herald, Dublin, Ireland; Dundee University Archives, Dundee, Scotland; Dumfries and Galloway Health Board Archives, Dumfries, Scotland; Lothian Health Service Archive, Edinburgh University Library, Edinburgh, Scotland; Northern Health Services Archive, Woolmanhill, Aberdeen, Scotland; Central Library, Guildhall Square, Portsmouth, England; Poole Central Library, Poole, Dorset, England; British Medical Association, Records and Archives, Tavistock Square, London; Cumbria Record Office, Kendal, Cumbria; Local Studies Archive, Oldmeldrum, Aberdeenshire; Aberdeen & North-East Scotland Family History Society; Aberdeenshire Library and Information Service; Royal Commission on the Ancient and Historical Monuments of Scotland.

Dr Allan Beveridge; Geraint Bowen; Nellie Carr; James and Carol Ince; Joyce Irvine; Judith Legg; Donald McCaskill; Rosie McLure; Steven Powrie; Peter Tewksbury; Fiona R. Watson; Morag Williams; Louise Yeoman; Dr Mary Young; Daniel Parker; Alice Grayson; Kristina Watson.

I wish, most sincerely, to thank Scirard R. Lancelyn Green for the use of photographs from the collection of the late Richard Lancelyn Green. This collection has been donated to Portsmouth City Council, where an exhibition of it may be seen at the City Museum and Records Office. As regards photographs credited to Paddington Press, despite strenuous efforts it has not been possible to trace this publishing house, which appears to be defunct.

I am especially grateful to my dear wife Rachel, for her help and encouragement.

# Preface

It is the year 1900 and Arthur Conan Doyle, now aged forty-one, is at the height of his powers. A qualified doctor who has travelled widely; a keen and able sportsman who once bowled out the legendary Dr W.G. Grace in a cricket match (a favour which the great cricketer was quick to return!); a chronicler of the South African War (which he witnessed at first hand); a writer of historical novels and patriotic pamphlets, and a champion of the oppressed and the underdog. Most of all, however, he is known for being the creator of that honourable, brave, scientific, and eminently sensible master detective Sherlock Holmes.

Every new Holmes story is greeted with great anticipation and confidence in the knowledge that however complex the crime, the eminently intelligent and logical Holmes will solve it. It therefore comes as a great surprise to his readers, when in the year 1916, the author, now Sir Arthur (he was knighted in 1902), declares that he believes in spiritualism. How can the creator of the inexorably logical Sherlock Holmes behave like this? It simply does not add up. And when, in 1922, Doyle publishes a book in which he professes to believe in fairies, the vast majority of his devotees are, frankly, nonplussed. For many, this was too much. Suddenly the iconic figure of Doyle instead becomes a figure of fun; a subject of ridicule, mirth, and derision.

Having an enquiring mind like Doyle, I was prompted to ask what he was seeking when he renounced his former Roman Catholic religion and became a spiritualist. Was there something lacking in his life which led him into an investigation of the paranormal? As for believing in fairies, this seemed altogether too bizarre. So how could one account for it?

As I commenced my research my first instinct was to empathise with Doyle, not for his strange beliefs, but for the reason that like him I am a former medical practitioner who became a writer (in my case, following a spinal injury). What if he had walked into my former surgery in Poole, Dorset (his being in Southsea, Hampshire) one day as a patient, and told me his story? Perhaps, the first thing I should have asked him, discreetly of course, would have been if there were any other members of the Doyle family who had had similar experiences? Unfortunately, for obvious reasons, it is impossible for me to question Doyle himself.

Nonetheless, when I came to investigate Doyle's psyche using his own writings (both factual and fictional) as my predominant source, I found the journey just as exciting as any of the cases embarked upon by the great Sherlock Holmes, and all the more extraordinary because this was *real life*! Like Holmes, I was now looking for clues which I largely found subtly concealed in Doyle's own writings.

The trail led to Scotland, to the remote hamlet of Blairerno near the east coast; to Montrose; to Edinburgh; and to Dumfries. In all of these places Doyle's father, Charles Altamont, had been forcibly incarcerated in various institutions for both his own safety and for that of others. Could it be that Charles held the key to the unanswered questions about his son?

My investigations led me to conclude that Doyle's father had suffered not only from alcoholism and epilepsy, as has previously been described, but more importantly from a serious mental illness. Not only that, but this illness was itself a hereditable disease, in other words, one which Charles may have handed down to his son via the genes. Suddenly I realised that I now had an opportunity to solve what I consider to be the ultimate mystery, that of the bizarre and extraordinary nature of Sir Arthur Conan Doyle himself!

# I

# Formative Years
and Influences

Arthur Ignatius Conan Doyle (hereafter called Doyle) was born on 22 May 1859 at 11 Picardy Place, Edinburgh, of Irish Catholic parents. He was the third of nine children, and the eldest son.

Doyle's son Adrian states that on his father's side, Doyle was descended from, 'a line of Irish country squires' who were Catholics and landed gentry.[1] However, life for them would not be easy when, as Doyle states, with the coming of the Reformation (the rejection of the authority of the Roman Catholic Church), 'My forebears, like most old Irish families in the south [of Ireland] kept to the old faith [i.e. Roman Catholicism] … and fell victim to the penal laws [which were designed to prevent Catholics from achieving wealth and power] in consequence.'[2] The outcome was that, in 1668, Doyle's great-great-great-great-grandfather John Doyle:

> …was dispossessed of almost all his Irish land in favour of the Duke of York; only the small estate of Barracurra was left him, and his grandson Richard was forced to leave even this in 1762. After being uprooted from his home, Richard went to Dublin and set up as a silk merchant. His son James Doyle had two sons, of whom the elder John [grandfather of Doyle], was born in 1797.[3]

Doyle's grandfather John showed an early talent for painting and drawing – his favourite subject being horses – for which he received many commissions. In 1820 he married Marianna Conan, whose father was a Dublin tailor, like her husband's father. Marianna is described as, '… the surviving cadet of the Conan family [from whom Doyle derives his middle name], the ancient ducal House of Brittany,' who fled to Ireland following the religious persecution of her forebears.[4]

In 1821 or 1822, John and Marianna, who by now had a baby daughter Ann Martha ('Annette'), moved to London. Here John continued in his career as a painter, exhibiting regularly at the Royal Academy between 1825 and 1850. He later became a political satirist and cartoonist. Next came James Edmund William (b.1822); Richard (b.1824); Henry Edward (b.1827); Francis (b.1829, 'Frank', who died aged fifteen); Adelaide (b.1831, who died of tuberculosis in 1844); and finally, Charles Altamont (b.1832). In 1833 the Doyle family took up residence at 17 Cambridge Terrace in the fashionable district to the north of Hyde Park.

James became an illustrator of books, an antiquary and the author of *The Historical Baronage of England* and *A Chronicle of England* (which he illustrated in colour). Richard became an illustrator and watercolour painter with a fascination for fairy tales and legends. He also worked for seven years for the satirical magazine *Punch*. Henry became director of the National Gallery of Ireland, founder of the National Historical and Portrait Gallery and designer of religious murals. As for Charles Altamont, his story is as follows.

A vacancy arose at the Scottish Office of Works in 1849 and Charles moved to Edinburgh to become one of the assistants to Robert Matheson, Chief Surveyor for Scotland. Here in the Scottish capital, Charles eventually came to lodge with Katherine (née Pack), widow of Dr William Foley of Trinity College, Dublin, and a descendant of the Percy family of Northumberland. In July 1855, Charles married his landlady's elder daughter Mary Josephine Foley in Edinburgh's Roman Catholic Cathedral of St Mary.

The couple went on to have nine children: Anne Mary Frances Conan (b.1856, known as 'Annette'); Catherine Amelia Angela (b.1858, but died in the same year of hydrocephalus). On 22 May 1859, arrived Arthur Ignatius Conan, the principal subject of this narrative, who derived his second name from the fact that his parents were married on 31 July, the Feast of St Ignatius; Mary Helena Monica Henrietta (b.1861, died of laryngitis aged two years;[5] Caroline Mary Burton (1866, 'Lottie'); Constance Amelia Monica (b.1868, 'Connie'); John Francis Innes Hay (b.1873, 'Innes'); Jane Adelaide Rose (b.1875, 'Ida'); Bryan Mary Julia Josephine (b.1877, 'Dodo').

To supplement his income and provide for the growing family, Charles devoted his spare time to producing the illustrations for fourteen books, including John Bunyan's allegory *Pilgrim's Progress* and Daniel Defoe's *The Life and Surprising Adventures of Robinson Crusoe*. Magazines which he illustrated included *Diogenes*, *The Illustrated Times*, *Good Words*, *London Society*, and *The Graphic*. He also painted: favourite subjects being landscapes of Scotland, humorous cartoons and fairies. He also worked as a sketch artist in criminal trials. In 1876, Charles was promoted in the Scottish Office of Works to become second assistant surveyor out of three.

★   ★   ★

In 1868, when he was aged nine years, Doyle was sent away to boarding school for his education: first to Hodder Preparatory School in Lancashire and then on to the adjacent Roman Catholic public school of Stonyhurst. The fees were paid, not by his impecunious father, but by his more prosperous uncles. Now, 'save for six weeks each summer, one never left the school,' said Doyle.[6] Allegedly, this was to keep him away from his father Charles who had become heavily dependent on alcohol.

In 1874, the fifteen year old Doyle travelled to London for the first time where he visited his uncle Richard Doyle, the illustrator and watercolour painter. Four years previously, Richard had published his most famous book *In Fairyland*. He and Doyle now

> became firm friends, and Dick [Richard] entertained his nephew by showing him his studio, full of paintings and drawings of goblins and fairies, elves and ghosts, dragons and witches. He also told young Arthur [Doyle] some of his favourite stories of fairies and ghosts and legends, thoroughly indoctrinating him into the 'other world' which also captivated Arthur's father.[7]

Forty-six years later, the subject of fairies would again impinge on Doyle's life, and this time in a most dramatic way.

★   ★   ★

Charles's alcoholism would have immense implications for the family in the years to come. At that time, the view of the medical profession was epitomised by Professor John Glaister in his work *A Text-Book of Medical Jurisprudence and Toxicology* first published in the year 1921. Glaister acknowledged that '… insanity – perhaps of a temporary kind – may be induced by the direct effects of alcohol.'

Glaister also stated that, '... alcoholism is one of the more indirect causes of the insane condition ....'[8] However, had Charles been examined by a present day psychiatrist, the question asked might well have been, could the reverse of this proposition by Glaister have been the case i.e. did Charles have a pre-existing mental condition which predisposed him to alcoholism? This will be discussed in more detail later.

As for Doyle, his final year of schooling was spent at a Jesuit school in Austria. It was during his schooldays that he renounced his belief in Roman Catholicism.

# From Doctor to Writer: Sherlock Holmes

Perhaps it was at the suggestion of Bryan Charles Waller, who came to lodge with Charles Doyle and his family in about 1875 and became their benefactor, that Doyle decided to become a doctor. Waller himself had arrived in Edinburgh in 1871 to take up the study of medicine. In any event, Doyle entered Edinburgh University's medical school in 1876 where he met the thirty-nine year old Dr Joseph Bell, author of *A Manual of the Operations of Surgery*. It was ironic that although Bell was Doyle's medical mentor, it was he who would set the latter on the road to becoming a writer, as will shortly be seen.

In his autobiography, Doyle described how Dr Bell (who paid Doyle the compliment of making him his out-patient clerk), '…often learned more of the patient by a few quick glances than I had done by my questions.[1] If he [Bell] were a detective, he would surely reduce this fascinating but unorganised business to something nearer to an exact science. I would try if I could get this effect. It was surely possible in real life, so why should I not make it plausible in fiction?'[2]

Whilst still a medical student Doyle worked for a while as assistant to Dr Richardson of Sheffield, Dr Elliott of Shropshire and to Dr Hoare of Birmingham where his duties included the making up of prescriptions. It was then, he said, 'that I first learned that shillings might be earned in other ways than by filling phials. Some friend remarked to me that my letters were very vivid and surely I could write some things to sell.'[3]

Also during his time as a medical student Doyle sent his story *The Haunted Grange of Goresthorpe*, described by him as 'a true ghost story', to Blackwood's *Edinburgh Magazine*. They declined to publish it.

Undeterred, he sent *The Mystery of the Sasassa Valley*, a story set in South Africa and involving a treasure-hunt, to Edinburgh's *Chambers's Journal* which published it on 6 September 1879. In the same month, an academic article by him entitled *Gelseminum as a Poison* appeared in the *British Medical Journal*. (He had first-hand knowledge of Gelseminum which is derived from the root of jasmine, having used it to treat himself for an attack of neuralgia).

Meanwhile, back at home Mary Doyle was undergoing what Doyle described as 'the long, sordid strain' of having to cope with her husband Charles,[4] who was forced to retire from the Scottish Office of Works in 1876. He now found himself having to live on a pension that was inadequate to support his family.[5] Nevertheless, he appears to have continued his work as a book illustrator. No less than sixty of his illustrations appeared in Jean Jambon's *Our Trip to Blunderland* (a parody of Lewis Carroll's *Alice's Adventures in Wonderland*, published in 1877 by William Blackwood & Sons, of which 15,000 copies were printed in the first two years).

Finally, the problem of Charles's continued heavy drinking coupled with his increasing 'bouts of melancholia and depression'[6] proved too great for the family to bear and in 1879, at the age of forty-seven[7] he was admitted to Blairerno House, a home for intemperates (those given to excessive indulgence in alcohol), situated seventy miles from his home town of Edinburgh and near the village of Drumlithie in Aberdeenshire (then Kincardineshire), north-east Scotland. Charles would now spend the remainder of his days in one institution or another. As for his wife Mary and their children – including Doyle (Arthur), now aged twenty, it is doubtful whether they ever saw him again.

\*  \*  \*

Doyle's world was not confined to that of writing and medicine. In 1880, for example, the year before he qualified, he served 'in the capacity of surgeon' for seven months on the 200 ton whaling vessel *Hope* of Peterhead, in the 'Arctic Seas'.[8] From October 1881, he served for three months as surgeon on the 400 ton steamer *Mayumba* to West Africa: experiences which resulted in him including seafaring tales amongst the short stories which he was now writing. During these varied experiences and others which followed later, Doyle was furnishing his mind with material which would find its way into his writings both fictional and non-fictional. For example, a visit to Liberia had given him an insight into the brutality of the slave trade which had existed there; his indignation being reflected in *The Crime of the Congo*, published in 1909, which described in graphic detail the oppression by the Belgian colonists of the native Congolese. Doyle's seafaring trips also provided inspiration for *J. Habakuk Jephson's Statement* (1883), in which a possible solution to the mystery of the *Marie Celeste* (an American brigantine found abandoned with sails set between Portugal and The Azores in 1872) is offered.

In August 1881, Doyle graduated from Edinburgh as Bachelor of Medicine and Master of Surgery.[9] Having qualified, he worked as a general practitioner in Plymouth and then from June 1882 in Southsea, Portsmouth. At this latter place he decided that producing novels would be more financially remunerative than short stories and to this end he commenced *The Narrative of John Smith*, described by him as being 'of a personal-social-political complexion' and 'perilously near the libellous'.[10] Unfortunately, his only copy of the manuscript of this work was lost en route to the publisher. He then commenced writing another story (this time semi-autobiographical and featuring Edinburgh University) which would finally be entitled *The Firm of Girdlestone* (1890).

In November 1883, Doyle became a member of the Portsmouth Literary and Scientific Society, which brought him into contact with General Alfred Drayson, whom he described as 'a very distinguished thinker and a pioneer of psychic knowledge …'.[11] It was Drayson who introduced him to theosophy (a theosophist being one who claims to receive divine illumination or inspiration, and to have abnormal control over natural forces). Drayson told Doyle that the fundamental truth was 'that every spirit in the flesh passes over to the next world exactly as it is, with no change whatsoever.'[12] These words made a great impression on Doyle, now aged twenty-four, to the extent that he adopted this tenet of Drayson's for himself as one, and perhaps the most important, of his core beliefs. Doyle also played football, keeping goal for a team which later became Portsmouth City Football Club.

In late 1883, Mary Doyle, together with children Connie, Ida, Dodo, and Innes, moved to Masongill in North Yorkshire to a cottage on the estate belonging to the family of Bryan Waller, Mary's former lodger.[13] Waller had retired to Masongill the previous year (having inherited the estate on the death of his father in 1877), and had now given up his medical career. Waller was aware of Mary's plight, and had helped the family financially. It was probably as a result of his benevolence that Mary gave her youngest daughter the somewhat inappropriate first name of Bryan.

In 1885, Doyle obtained his doctorate, also from Edinburgh, on aspects of the venereal disease syphilis. In that year, a widow Mrs Emily Hawkins, her son John and her daughter Louise became Doyle's patients, having arrived in Southsea from Gloucester. When Jack, aged twenty-five, contracted meningitis Doyle took him into his own lodgings to care for him. The attempt, however, was unsuccessful and the boy died. Doyle subsequently developed a friendship with Louise, whom he married on 6 August of that year. He was aged twenty-six and she twenty-eight. To supplement his income Doyle continued with his short story writing for which he was paid, '£4 on average'.[14]

On 26 May 1885, shortly before Doyle's wedding, his father Charles managed to acquire some liquor; became violent and attempted to leave Blairerno House by breaking a window. This, apparently, was not the first time he had attempted to break free from there.[15] In consequence, he was transferred to the Montrose Royal Asylum ('Sunnyside' wing). Here he was held under a detention order as a lunatic, this being defined as

> … any mad or furious or fatuous [vacant, silly, purposeless, or idiotic] person, or person so diseased or affected in mind as to render him unfit in the opinion of competent medical persons to be at large, either as regards his own personal safety and conduct, or the safety of the persons and property of others or of the public.[16]

How distressing it must have been for Doyle and his family to hear Charles described in this way.

★  ★  ★

Meanwhile, a breakthrough for Doyle came in 1887 with *A Study in Scarlet* where Sherlock Holmes and Dr Watson appear for the first time. This story, illustrated by Doyle's father Charles who depicted Sherlock Holmes uniquely sporting a beard, was published in *Beeton's Christmas Annual* of that year. Others to take Doyle's work included the *Pall Mall Gazette*, *The Cornhill*, and *Lippincott's Magazine*.

The plot for *The Mystery of Cloomber* (1888) arose out of Doyle's meeting in Southsea with the spiritualist General A. W. Drayson. In this story, Doyle (in contrast to Sherlock Holmes) presents a sceptical view of science: an indication that he had become disillusioned with the subject:

...history has shown that it [science] is slow to accept a truth. Science sneered at Newton for twenty years. Science proved mathematically that an iron ship could not swim, and science declared that a steam ship could not cross the Atlantic.[17]

In January 1889, Doyle and his wife Louise's first child was born, a daughter Mary Louise. Now came two historical novels: *Micah Clarke* set during the time of the Monmouth Rebellion of 1685, which was published that year and *The White Company*, a story of English mercenary soldiers operating in France and Spain in the fourteenth century and published in 1890. That year began with the tragic death in Portugal from influenza of Doyle's sister Annette.

Doyle's work as a family doctor, together with his writing, did not prevent him from taking a lively interest in the medical topic of the day – even to the extent of becoming personally involved. In August 1890, Robert Koch, German physician and discoverer of the tubercle bacillus which causes tuberculosis, announced to the International Medical Congress of Berlin that a drug which he had produced, tuberculin, was a cure for tuberculosis. Doyle, was not so sure however, it being his view that 'the whole thing was experimental and premature'.[18] Doyle was proved right. Tuberculin, although useful in diagnosis of tuberculosis, was ineffective as a cure. There was a sad irony in the fact of Doyle's especial interest in tuberculosis, bearing in mind the fate that was to befall his wife Louise, as will shortly be demonstrated.

In March 1891, the family moved to London where Doyle hoped to become an eye specialist. Here they rented rooms, first at 23 Montague Place, Bloomsbury and subsequently from June, at 12 Tennison Road, South Norwood on the fringes of Greater London.

In July 1891, short stories involving detective Sherlock Holmes and his associate Dr John Watson, began to appear regularly in *The Strand Magazine* which caused the newly founded publication's circulation to almost double. Doyle was now commissioned to write a further six stories following the first series, and then a further twelve. He soon found himself in a position to embark on a career of full-time writing, during the course of which he would write several historical novels. For example, *A Straggler of '15* (1891) describes the final days of a veteran of Waterloo. It was subsequently performed as the one-act play *Waterloo* (1895), starring the legendary actor Henry Irving. However, although he would not have wished it, it is for

Sherlock Holmes that Doyle is best remembered, for it was his legendary detective who would set him on the path to fame and fortune.

In the preface to *Sherlock Holmes: The Long Stories*, Doyle states that, 'Having endured a severe course of training in medical diagnosis, I felt that if the same austere methods of observation and reasoning were applied to the problems of crime some more scientific system could be constructed.' Doyle would later give credit where it was due by dedicating his story *The Adventures of Sherlock Holmes* 'To my old teacher Joseph Bell, MD &c. of 2 Melville Crescent, Edinburgh.' As for Holmes, he become not only a household name, but in the eyes of the public *a very real person*! Doyle himself acknowledged this, saying in later years

> Well, the curious thing is, how many people there are in the world who are perfectly convinced that he is a living human being. I get letters addressed to him. I get letters asking for his autograph. I get letters addressed to his rather stupid friend Watson. I've even had ladies writing to say that they would be very glad to act as his housekeeper.[19]

★   ★   ★

In the summer of 1892, the Doyles, together with Doyle's sister Connie, visited Norway in company with author Jerome K. Jerome. In November that year, the couple had a son Arthur Alleyne Kingsley (known as Kingsley). Meanwhile, *The Great Shadow* (1892), describes the crisis leading to the Battle of Waterloo through the eyes of a Scottish boy.

# 3

# Doyle Sets the Scene

The address 221B Baker Street is situated in a fashionable district of London to the south of Regent's Park, and this is the place where so many of the Sherlock Holmes stories begin, and end. It is morning. Dr John H. Watson is reading the newspaper; Holmes is puffing on his tobacco pipe and occasionally evoking a few discordant sounds from his violin. He sometimes looks wistfully out of the window at urchins playing in the street below and at horse drawn carriages clattering by as he wonders what the day will bring. And of course, there is always Mrs Hudson to provide a meal or a tray of tea: something which Watson always appreciates, although Holmes views eating as more of a necessity than a pleasure. Holmes is intensely motivated by the desire for mental stimulation, and this is reflected in the following words to his chronicler and colleague Dr Watson:

> I know, my dear Watson, that you share my love of all that is bizarre and outside the conventions and humdrum routine of everyday life. You have shown your relish for it by the enthusiasm which has prompted you to chronicle, and, if you will excuse my saying so, somewhat to embellish so many of my own little adventures. (*The Red-headed League*)

From this, Doyle's readers are immediately aware that before very long Holmes' passionate thirst for excitement and adventure – along with their own – will soon be requited! Doyle whets the appetite of his readers further by having Holmes declare that 'For strange effects and extraordinary combinations, we must go to life itself, which is always far more daring than any effort of the imagination,' (*The Red-headed League*).

So how do Holmes' clients come to arrive at 221B Baker Street? The answer is, in a variety of ways. Their first approach may be made by letter, often unsigned and unaddressed; or they may appear on the doorstep either by prior appointment or sometimes unannounced – much to housekeeper Mrs Hudson's consternation – at the apartment. Or, it may be that Watson draws Holmes' attention to a particularly intriguing case, reports of which he has read in the newspapers. One or other of them may even observe a confrontation, a crime or some unusual event in the street. Or, as is often the case, some police inspector who knows of Holmes' reputation arrives, anxious to enlist his support in the solving of a particularly baffling crime.

For his part, Holmes is always careful to understate his desire to become involved in a new case but if remotely tempted, he offers encouragement by employing one of his favourite sayings; 'The case has certainly some points of interest.' This is another device by which Doyle keeps his readers on tenterhooks: will the great detective accept the challenge or will he not?

Having come face to face with a potential client Holmes has a habit of demurring that person's first request, however illustrious he or she may be. Is this case sufficiently intriguing to merit his attention, he asks himself and is it likely that he will be adequately rewarded for his pains? For yes, money to Holmes is certainly a consideration. Of course, if the client declares the affair to be of national importance and appeals to his sense of patriotism then it is likely that he will be persuaded to take on the case. For example, in *The Adventure of the Second Stain* Watson describes an occasion when

> … we found two visitors of European fame within the walls of our humble room in Baker Street. The one, austere, high-nosed, eagle-eyed, and dominant, was none other than the illustrious Lord Bellinger, twice Premier of Britain. The other, dark, clear-cut, and elegant, hardly yet of middle-age, and endowed with every beauty of body and of mind, was the Right Honourable Trelawney Hope, Secretary for European Affairs, and the most rising statesman in the country.

They have come to Baker Street to persuade Holmes to retrieve a document which has gone missing: one which the Premier tells him is '… of such immense importance that its publication might very easily – I might almost say probably – lead to European complications of the utmost moment. It is not too much to say that peace or war may hang upon the issue.' However, when the Premier refuses to divulge the contents of the document to

Holmes – on the grounds of secrecy – the latter behaves in characteristic fashion, by rising from his seat and saying 'You are two of the most busy men in the country, and in my own small way I have also a good many calls upon me. I regret exceedingly that I cannot help you in this matter, and any continuation of this interview would be a waste of time.'

Is this possible? Is Holmes *really* going to turn down a request by the Premier of Britain himself? By this time Doyle's readers are anxiously sitting up in their seats! The matter is finally resolved, only when the two statesmen appeal to Holmes' sense of honour and patriotism. He then agrees to take on the case.

In *The Red-headed League* Watson describes how he and Holmes are visiting a concert hall where the music enables the latter thoroughly to relax prior to galvanizing himself for action:

> My friend was an enthusiastic musician, being himself not only a very capable performer but a composer of no ordinary merit. All the afternoon he sat in the stalls wrapped in the most perfect happiness, gently waving his long, thin fingers in time to the music, while his gently smiling face and his languid, dreamy eyes were as unlike those of Holmes, the sleuth-hound, Holmes the relentless, keen-witted, ready-handed criminal agent, as it was possible to conceive. In his singular character the dual nature alternately asserted itself, and his extreme exactness and astuteness represented, as I have often thought, the reaction against the poetic and contemplative mood which occasionally predominated in him. The swing of his nature took him from extreme languor to devouring energy; and, as I knew well, he was never so truly formidable as when, for days on end, he had been lounging in his armchair amid his improvisations and his black-letter editions. Then it was that the lust of the chase would suddenly come upon him, and that his brilliant reasoning power would rise to the level of intuition, until those who were unacquainted with his methods would look askance at him as on a man whose knowledge was not that of other mortals. When I saw him that afternoon so enwrapped in the music at St. James's Hall I felt that an evil time might be coming upon those whom he had set himself to hunt down. (*The Red-headed League*)

The analogy between Holmes and a tiger in the jungle, which sleeps after eating until he is replete and then awakens hungry for the next kill, would seem apt, given the following description of him given by Watson in *The Boscombe Valley Mystery*. Here Holmes is attempting to identify the murderer of tenant farmer Charles McCarthy:

> Sherlock Holmes was transformed when he was hot upon such a scent as this. Men who had only known the quiet thinker and logician of Baker Street would have failed to recognize him. His face flushed and darkened. His brows were drawn into two hard black lines, while his eyes shone out from beneath them with a steely glitter. His face was bent downwards, his shoulders bowed, his lips compressed, and the veins stood out like whipcord in his long, sinewy neck. His nostrils seemed to dilate with a purely animal lust for the chase, and his mind was so absolutely concentrated upon the matter before him that a question or remark fell unheeded upon his ears, or, at the most, only provoked a quick, impatient snarl in reply.

When it comes to power of observation, Holmes undoubtedly has no peer. However, when it comes to giving an impartial and detailed description of the great detective, Watson for once has the upper hand.

* * *

In Sherlock Holmes, Doyle had created, arguably, the world's most famous detective. So what ingredients went into the make-up of this fictional character, such that he would become a household word name right around the globe? How did Doyle portray him so as to make his image so easily recognisable in his readers' minds? The answer is twofold. Firstly, Holmes demonstrates many qualities with which Doyle's readers will immediately identify, and secondly, he has others, which they find not only puzzling but also intriguing.

Perhaps the first image to come to mind at the mention of Sherlock Holmes, is a man in a deerstalker hat, smoking a large pipe of tobacco which for some reason enables him both to relax and think at the same time. This is demonstrated in the mystery of *The Red-headed League*, where Holmes tells Watson that he intends to have a smoke:

> 'It is quite a three-pipe problem, and I beg that you won't speak to me for fifty minutes.' He curled himself up in his chair, with his thin knees

drawn up to his hawk-like nose, and there he sat with his eyes closed and his black clay pipe thrusting out like the bill of some strange bird.

In *The Adventure of the Copper Beeches,* Holmes makes it clear to Watson how, even when he has the opportunity of relaxing, his mind is always focussed on the task in hand. The two are travelling together by train through the countryside of southern England. 'Are they not fresh and beautiful?' cries Watson, admiring 'the little red and grey roofs of the farm-steadings' and 'the light green of the new foliage.' Holmes however, sees things in a very different light:

Do you know, Watson, that it is one of the curses of a mind with a turn like mine that I must look at everything with reference to my own special subject. You look at these scattered houses, and you are impressed by their beauty. I look at them, and the only thought which comes to me is a feeling of their isolation and of the impunity with which crime may be committed there.

In fact it was Holmes' belief that '… the lowest and vilest alleys in London do not present a more dreadful record of sin than does the smiling and beautiful countryside.' And why? Simply because of its isolation, 'Think of the deeds of hellish cruelty, the hidden wickedness which may go on, year in, year out, in such places, and none the wiser.' People to whom work is a vocation, an obsession even, might well empathise with Holmes as he expresses those sentiments. They might also understand how when work is going well, Holmes feels cheerful and when it is going badly, he does not. In fact, as the result of long experience Dr Watson, his companion and chronicler, could deduce from Holmes' behaviour how well or badly a case was progressing. In *The Adventure of the Second Stain*, for example, he describes a day when:

… Holmes was in a mood which his friends would call taciturn, and others morose. He ran out and ran in, smoked incessantly, played snatches on his violin, sank into reveries, devoured sandwiches at irregular hours, and hardly answered the casual questions which I put to him. It was evident to me that things were not going well with him or his quest.

Holmes was perhaps ahead of time in his refusal to be polite to those for whom he had little or no respect. In *A Scandal in Bohemia,* he is instrumental in retrieving a compromising photograph from the beautiful Irene Adler, described as 'an adventuress', in order to save the reputation of Bohemia's King Wilhelm, whom he evidently despises. This is apparent at the end of the story when Watson describes Holmes' final words to the king thus:

> 'I thank your Majesty. Then there is no more to be done in the matter. I have the honour to wish you a very good-morning.' He bowed, and, turning away without observing the hand which the King had stretched out to him, he set off in my company for his chambers.

Another reason why Doyle's readers are able to empathise with Holmes is that, generally speaking, the people to whom he chooses to come to the aid of are those who find themselves, for some reason not of their making, placed at a disadvantage, often having been wrongly accused of committing a crime. In his later years, Doyle was to employ the same gifts of detection as he had imbued Holmes with – to champion the cause of some real life people who had been unfortunate enough to suffer the experience of wrongful conviction in the courts, as will later be seen.

The other side of the coin and the one which is perhaps even more fascinating for Holmes' followers and devotees, is the fact that he is an enigmatic character who leads an idiosyncratic lifestyle. Perhaps Holmes demonstrates this most clearly in his attitude towards women, for as Watson states, he appears to have no interest in the female sex, other than in a professional capacity – all emotions, and particularly that of romantic love, being:

> … particularly … abhorrent to his cold, precise but admirably balanced mind… as a lover he would have placed himself in a false position. He never spoke of the softer passions, save with a gibe and a sneer. They were admirable things for the observer— excellent for drawing the veil from men's motives and actions. But for the trained reasoner to admit such intrusions into his own delicate and finely adjusted temperament, was to introduce a distracting factor which might throw a doubt upon all his mental results.

There was, however, one woman of whom he made an exception. This was Irene Adler from *A Scandal in Bohemia*. 'In his eyes she eclipses and predominates the whole of her sex.'

In *The Adventure of the Second Stain*, Lady Hilda Trelawney Hope, who Holmes later suspects of removing an important document from the dispatch box of her husband, the Secretary for European Affairs, without his knowledge or consent, pays a visit to Baker Street. As she leaves, she implores Holmes and Watson to say nothing of this visit to her husband. Nonetheless, the latter is profoundly impressed with their female visitor:, She looked back at us from the door, and I had a last impression of that beautiful, haunted face, the startled eyes, and the drawn mouth. Then she was gone.' Whereas Watson is smitten, the great detective makes it clear that he is not. 'Now, Watson, the fair sex is your department,' said Holmes, with a smile, when the dwindling frou-frou [rustling] of skirts had ended in the slam of the door. Being at first unable to ascertain the true purpose of Lady Hilda's visit, Holmes then goes on to make further observations on the fair sex in general, declaring to Watson, '… the motives of women are so inscrutable … How can you build on such a quicksand? Their most trivial action may mean volumes, or their most extraordinary conduct may depend upon a hairpin or a curling tong.'

When in *The Sign of Four* Watson falls in love with a Miss Mary Morstan, daughter of an officer who had served in the army in India, and tells Holmes, 'I fear that it may be the last investigation in which I shall have the chance of studying your methods. Miss Morstan has done me the honour to accept me as a husband in prospective.' Holmes' reaction is entirely predictable. He gives a dismal groan and says:, 'I feared as much. I really cannot congratulate you.' Nevertheless, Holmes is prepared to concede that Miss Morstan:

> … is one of the most charming young ladies I ever met, and might have been most useful in such work as we have been doing … . But love is an emotional thing, and whatever is emotional is opposed to that true, cold reason which I place above all things. I should never marry myself, lest I bias my judgment.

4

# Doyle and Holmes:
# Analogous Lives

A part from those already mentioned, Doyle's historical and romantic novels would shortly include amongst others: *Round the Red Lamp*, 1894 (a collection of medical stories); *The Lord of Chateau Noir*, 1894 (French guerrilla warfare following the Franco-Prussian War of 1870-1); *Rodney Stone*, 1896 (historical novel set during the time of the Regency and featuring prize-fighting); *The Green Flag,* 1900 (Irish mutiny in the British army in the 1880s). His continued interest in the Napoleonic era was reflected in the *Brigadier Gerard* stories, composed between 1894 and 1903 (presenting a view of Napoleon's Europe).

Naturally, with works such as these, the creation of which he regarded as being his forte, Doyle felt that he had every reason to believe that this is what he would best be remembered for. However, it was not to be; for much to his chagrin, compared with the fame achieved by his Sherlock Holmes novels, everything else would pale into insignificance.

There are many similarities between the life of a medical practitioner and that of a crime investigator. As a doctor Doyle would have used a magnifying glass to examine skin rashes and blemishes, whereas Holmes might have used the same object for examining, say, a fingerprint. Whereas Doyle would have used a microscope for examining blood or bodily secretions, so Holmes might have used one for examining samples of human hair or textiles. Doyle would have been familiar with the test tube and the Bunsen burner, which Holmes would have used to perform his chemical analyses of forensic specimens. For example, in *The Adventure of the Dancing Men* Holmes is described as sitting for some long hours in silence, with his long, thin back curved over a chemical vessel in which he was brewing a particularly malodorous product.

Just as Doyle, as a hospital doctor, had a paper published in the *British Medical Journal* and would undoubtedly have published many more had he remained in the medical profession, so Holmes wrote papers on a variety of subjects relevant to his work as a detective. For instance, in *The Sign of Four* Holmes refers Watson to a monograph of his entitled *Upon the Distinction Between the Ashes of the Various Tobaccos*:

In it I enumerate a hundred and forty forms of cigar, cigarette, and pipe tobacco, with coloured plates illustrating the difference in the ash. It is a point which is continually turning up in criminal trials, and which is sometimes of supreme importance as a clue.

He also refers to further monographs that he has written, such as *Upon the Tracing of Footsteps, with some Remarks upon the Uses of Plaster of Paris as a Preserver of Impresses*.

Whereas a family doctor might reasonably be expected to have an extensive knowledge of his patients and their ailments, so a good detective would have stored in his memory a knowledge of the criminal fraternity. For example, in *The Adventure of the Second Stain* when a valuable document goes missing from the dispatch box of the Right Honourable Trelawney Hope, Secretary for European Affairs, Holmes tells Watson that in his opinion there are only three people capable of 'playing so bold a game as to steal it [namely]: Oberstein, La Rothière, and Eduardo Lucas.'

In Doyle's day, the family doctor would have kept a file of notes, written out in longhand, for each and every patient. Likewise Holmes, who was wise enough to know that however retentive the human brain may be, it is also necessary to maintain a dossier of information, particularly in respect of known criminals. This he makes good use of in *A Scandal in Bohemia,* when he is investigating the 'well-known adventuress Irene Adler':

'Kindly look her up in my index, Doctor [Watson],' murmured Holmes without opening his eyes. For many years he had adopted a system of docketing all paragraphs concerning men and things, so that it was difficult to name a subject or a person on which he could not at once furnish information.

To which the good doctor swiftly replies:

'Born in New Jersey in the year 1858. Contralto... La Scala... Prima donna Imperial Opera of Warsaw – yes... Retired from operatic stage... Living in London.'

Finally, and most importantly, the prerequisites of both medicine and criminology are a thorough and meticulous observation and interrogation of the subject; a careful gathering together of the evidence; the putting forward of a scientific theory based on the findings and the testing of that theory to determine whether or not it is true. One of the secrets of Holmes' success is that he has a penchant for minutiae as is demonstrated in *The Adventure of the Priory School* when he sets himself the task of trying to find Heidegger, the German master at the Priory School who has gone missing. Watson and Holmes are searching a moor when in the middle of a pathway, 'clearly marked on the sodden soil, was the track of a bicycle.' The question is, does it belong to Heidegger? The answer is, no. Says Holmes:

A bicycle certainly, but not the bicycle. I am familiar with forty-two different impressions left by tyres. This, as you perceive, is a Dunlop, with a patch upon the outer cover. Heidegger's tyres were Palmer's, leaving longitudinal stripes. Aveling, the mathematical master, was sure upon the point. Therefore it is not Heidegger's track.

This was not the end of the story, for from the tracks left behind Holmes was also able to deduce in which direction the bicycle was travelling. He tells Watson:

'This track, as you perceive, was made by a rider who was going from the direction of the school.'

'Or towards it?'

'No, no, my dear Watson. The more deeply sunk impression is, of course, the hind wheel, upon which the weight rests. You perceive several places where it has passed across and obliterated the more shallow mark of the front one. It was undoubtedly heading away from the school.'

As a good doctor will compare his patient with others who have similar signs and symptoms when faced with a problem of diagnosis, so Holmes admits to using this type of lateral thinking to solve his own cases, as in *The Red-headed League*: 'As a rule, when I have heard some slight indication of the course of events, I am able to guide myself by the thousands of other similar cases which occur to my memory.' However, just as the results of a medical investigation may prove to be inconclusive, so may the same be true of a criminal investigation. It is therefore always necessary to keep an open mind and beware of circumstantial evidence which Holmes says is '… a very tricky thing. It may seem to point very straight to one thing, but if you shift your own point of view a little, you may find it pointing in an equally uncompromising manner to something entirely different.'

Holmes gives a fine account of his *modus operandi* in *The Boscombe Valley Mystery* where the body of the murdered ex-Australian tenant farmer Charles McCarthy is found 'stretched out upon the grass' beside a pool with his head 'beaten in by repeated blows of some heavy and blunt weapon.' Despite the seeming lack of evidence, and in particular the absence of any murder weapon, Holmes tells Inspector Lestrade of Scotland Yard that he believes the murderer of Charles McCarthy to be '… a tall man, left-handed, limps with the right leg, wears thick-soled shooting-boots and a grey cloak, smokes Indian cigars, uses a cigar-holder, and carries a blunt pen-knife in his pocket.' Needless to say, Holmes has managed to deduce all this by meticulously examining the scene of the crime – a wood near Boscombe Pool where the murdered man's body was discovered. This examination even extends to Holmes laying down 'upon his waterproof to have a better view' of the tracks which covered the ground around where the body had lain; 'turning over the leaves and dried sticks'; gathering up what seemed to Watson to be dust into an envelope and 'examining not only the ground but even the bark of a tree as far as he could reach.' Holmes tells Watson: 'You know my method. It is founded upon the observation of trifles.' As for the murdered man:

> 'His height I know that you might roughly judge from the length of his stride. His boots, too, might be told from their traces. Yes, they were peculiar boots.'
>
> 'But his lameness?'
>
> 'The impression of his right foot was always less distinct than his left. He put less weight upon it. Why? Because he limped – he was lame.'
>
> 'But his left-handedness.'
>
> 'You were yourself struck by the nature of the injury as recorded by the

surgeon at the inquest. The blow was struck from immediately behind, and yet was upon the left side. Now, how can that be unless it were by a left-handed man? He had stood behind that tree during the interview between the father and son. He had even smoked there. I found the ash of a cigar, which my special knowledge of tobacco ashes enables me to pronounce as an Indian cigar. I have, as you know, devoted some attention to this, and written a little monograph on the ashes of 140 different varieties of pipe, cigar, and cigarette tobacco. Having found the ash, I then looked round and discovered the stump among the moss where he had tossed it. It was an Indian cigar, of the variety which are rolled in Rotterdam.'

'And the cigar-holder?'

'I could see that the end had not been in his mouth. Therefore he used a holder. The tip had been cut off, not bitten off, but the cut was not a clean one, so I deduced a blunt pen-knife.'

These observations were made by the great Sherlock Holmes. They might equally well have been made by Dr Joseph Bell, Doyle's former tutor from the Edinburgh Medical School, had he chosen criminology rather than medicine as a profession.

Holmes is not averse to subjecting his colleague to the type of scrutiny that he would employ in solving a mystery. For example, in the same story, he astounds Watson by telling him that he believes the bedroom window of the latter's home to be 'upon the right-hand side … ' 'How on earth … ?' Says Holmes:

My dear fellow, I know you well. I know the military neatness which characterizes you. You shave every morning, and in this season you shave by the sunlight; but since your shaving is less and less complete as we get farther back on the left side, until it becomes positively slovenly as we get round the angle of the jaw, it is surely very clear that that side is less illuminated than the other. I only quote this as a trivial example of observation and inference. Therein lies my métier …

For all Holmes' brilliance, Doyle is not averse to taking him down a peg or two lest he become overly conceited as in *The Red-headed League*. Here Holmes makes certain deductions from the appearance of pawnbroker Mr Jabez Wilson, but is taken aback when the latter fails to be impressed, 'Well,

I never! I thought at first that you had done something clever, but I see that there was nothing in it, after all,' says Wilson. At which the mortified Holmes turns to Watson and says, 'I begin to think ... that I make a mistake in explaining [i.e. how he came to his conclusions]. *Omne ignotum pro magnifico* [Everything unfamiliar is magnified], you know, and my poor little reputation, such as it is, will suffer shipwreck if I am so candid.'

## 5

# Holmes Eclipses his Creator!

As already stated, Doyle always regarded his Sherlock Holmes stories as a necessary distraction from his main work which was writing historical novels, or later, chronicling great events such as the South African War. It therefore came as a great surprise to him, when following the publication of the first few Holmes stories in *The Strand Magazine*, Sherlock Holmes mania swept the country. When the circulation of that magazine practically doubled, its editor Herbert Greenhough Smith, made him an offer of £1,000 for a further series. Now, whereas many authors would have been ecstatic at the thought that a publisher was actually approaching *them* rather than vice versa, Doyle was frankly irritated. Not of course, by being offered the money but by the thought of having to write more Holmes stories – which would be a distraction from what he considered to be his more serious endeavours. After all, he was a great admirer of such literary eminences as Scottish novelist and poet the late Sir Walter Scott (1771-1832), whose style he copied in some of his early writings. As for the authors of detective fiction, his views on them and their creations can only be described as disdainful as this passage from *A Study in Scarlet* indicates. In the story, Dr Watson, who is meeting Sherlock Holmes for the very first time, declares of him, 'You remind me of Edgar Allan Poe's Dupin. [Poe – US poet, short story writer, and pioneer of modern detective fiction.] I had no idea that such individuals did exist outside of stories.' Holmes is far from being flattered by this comparison, and makes it clear that he regards Dupin with absolute contempt. 'No doubt you think that you are complimenting me in comparing me to Dupin. Now, in my opinion, Dupin was a very inferior fellow. He had some analytical genius, no doubt; but he was by no means such a phenomenon as Poe appeared to imagine.' Watson, not to be so easily defeated, now makes another attempt. 'Have you read Gaboriau's works? [French writer Emile Gaboriau] Does Lecoq come up to your idea of a detective?' (Lecoq being Gaboriau's fictional detective.) It is to no avail, for Holmes' reply is equally scathing:

> Lecoq was a miserable bungler. He had only one thing to recommend him, and that was his energy. That book made me positively ill. The question was how to identify an unknown prisoner. I could have done it in twenty-four hours. Lecoq took six months or so. It might be made a text-book for detectives to teach them what to avoid.

Aside from Holmes' intriguing character, his scrupulously meticulous gathering together of the evidence and his almost superhuman powers of deduction, what other factors came into play to make him compelling reading?

221B Baker Street, a first floor apartment in a fashionable district of London is not only the abode of Sherlock Holmes, it is also the nerve centre for Holmes' activities and the place where so many of the detective stories in which he features, start and finish. His companion is Dr Watson who somehow manages to combine the duties of a busy family doctor with that of recording the adventures of Sherlock Holmes in which he also participates.

It might be thought that Holmes would be flattered to have a chronicler, but on the contrary; for it is the habit of Holmes to criticise Watson (who is attempting to read the newspaper), for the way in which he has portrayed their latest case. Doyle commences so many of his Holmes stories in this way, with his two principal characters indulging in some friendly banter before settling down to the nitty-gritty of their next case. Doyle uses this simple domestic scene to familiarise his readers with the characters of both Holmes and Watson, while at the same time establishing their pecking order – Holmes invariably being the one in control. Doyle's readers, for their part, know from past experience that they are soon to share in a great adventure during which they expect to be intrigued, excited and even frightened. Yet they also know that at the end of it all Holmes and Watson will return to the safe environs of 221B Baker Street to take up where they left off until the next case beckons.

Whereas some of Holmes' clients are from relatively modest walks of life, a large number are from the higher echelons and in particular the aristocracy. Immediately therefore, the reader is led to believe that Holmes must be a good detective, otherwise why should such eminent people choose to consult him? For example, in *The Empty House* the murdered Honourable Ronald Adair is described as 'the second son of the Earl of Maynooth, at that time Governor of one of the Australian colonies. The youth moved in the best society … '

Holmes also proves himself more than a match for academics, no matter how many letters they may have after their names as in *The Adventure of the Priory School*. Here he is consulted by the founder and principal of that school Dr Thorneycroft Huxtable, M.A., Ph.D., who is also a classicist and the author of *Huxtable's Sidelights on Horace*. In fact, says Watson, the principal's card of introduction is seemingly 'too small to carry the weight of his academic distinctions … .' Says Dr Huxtable:

> The Priory is, without exception, the best and most select prepara-
> tory school in England. Lord Leverstoke, the Earl of Blackwater, Sir
> Cathcart Soames – they all have entrusted their sons to me. But I felt
> that my school had reached its zenith when, three weeks ago, the Duke
> of Holdernesse sent Mr James Wilder, his secretary, with the intimation
> that young Lord Saltire, ten years old, his only son and heir, was about
> to be committed to my charge.

Alas, the Duke's son has now been abducted; hence Dr Huxtable's visit to Baker Street to enlist the services of Holmes, who he hopes will discover the whereabouts of the missing pupil.

The headmaster informs Holmes that Heidegger, the German master at the school, has also gone missing along with his bicycle. However, when Dr Huxtable suggests, 'The bicycle may have been a blind. It may have been hidden somewhere, and the pair gone off on foot,' Holmes ridicules the idea:

> Quite so; but it seems rather an absurd blind, does it not? Were there
> other bicycles in this shed? Would he not have hidden a couple had he
> desired to give the idea that they had gone off upon them? Of course
> he would. The blind theory won't do.

In this way, Holmes proves his superiority over a learned academic by out-witting him even before the story has properly begun.

Holmes' status is further enhanced by Doyle's technique of building up his opponents in his reader's eyes, often making use of superlatives to describe their immense cunning and expertise. In this way, they are seen to constitute a challenge worthy of engaging the cerebral machinations of the great detective Sherlock Holmes. In *The Red-headed League* for example, Holmes quickly realises that a man calling himself Spaulding, who pawnbroker Mr Jabez Wilson has taken on as his new assistant, is in fact John Clay, a most ingenious criminal, 'Smart fellow, that. He is, in my judgment, the fourth smartest man in London, and for daring I am not sure that he has not a claim to be third.' Mr Jones of Scotland Yard duly arrives on the scene and enhances Clay's reputation even further by describing him as a:

> ... murderer, thief, smasher, and forger. He's a young man ... but he is at the head of his profession, and I would rather have my bracelets on him than on any criminal in London. He's a remarkable man, is young John Clay. His grandfather was a royal duke, and he himself has been to Eton and Oxford. His brain is as cunning as his fingers, and though we meet signs of him at every turn, we never know where to find the man himself. I've been on his track for years and have never set eyes on him yet.

The inference is, of course, that if Holmes can outwit such a man as John Clay – which of course he does – then Holmes must be *even cleverer* than the robber!

Doyle uses the same technique in *The Empty House*. Here, a Colonel Sebastian Moran is engaged in a plot to assassinate Holmes. The latter survives the attempt by placing an effigy of himself in his window at Baker Street to act as a decoy. When Moran is apprehended, Holmes describes him as, '... once of Her Majesty's Indian Army, and the best heavy game shot that our Eastern Empire has ever produced. I believe I am correct, Colonel, in saying that your bag of tigers still remains unrivalled?' As for the effigy, Holmes observes that, 'The old shikari's [hunter's] nerves have not lost their steadiness nor his eyes their keenness,' for the bullet had struck, 'plumb in the middle of the back of the head and [travelled] smack through the brain. He was the best shot in India, and I expect that there are few better in London.'

Perhaps the icing on the cake, so to speak, is when the police themselves express admiration for Holmes, and even on occasion enlist his help.

From this, the reader can only deduce that Holmes is also cleverer than the police, which is precisely what Doyle intends him or her to believe!

Holmes' relationship with the police force is normally a cordial one and because of their respect for his methods they usually permit him to work hand in hand with them. An example of such co-operation, not to say *bon-homie*, is apparent in *The Adventure of the Norwood Builder*, when Holmes requests that Inspector Lestrade gives him more time to interview a Mr John McFarlane who has just been arrested for murder. Lestrade replies: 'Well, Mr Holmes, it is difficult for me to refuse you anything, for you have been of use to the Force once or twice in the past, and we owe you a good turn at Scotland Yard.'

In private however, Holmes is not slow to voice his reservations – which sometimes amount to scorn – as in *The Red-headed League*, where he makes it clear to Watson why he has invited Mr Jones of Scotland Yard to join them. It is not on account of that policeman's mental prowess, 'I thought it as well to have Jones with us also. He is not a bad fellow, though an absolute imbecile in his profession. He has one positive virtue. He is as brave as a bulldog and as tenacious as a lobster if he gets his claws upon anyone.'

However, not all policemen are considered by Holmes to be dim or incompetent, a case in point being the young Stanley Hopkins who is described in *The Golden Pince-nez* as 'a promising detective, in whose career Holmes had several times shown a very practical interest'. Hopkins, who is investigating the case of the violent death of a secretary at a country house, admits to Holmes that he:

> …can make neither head nor tail of it. So far as I can see it is just as tangled a business as ever I handled, and yet at first it seemed so simple that one couldn't go wrong. There's no motive, Mr. Holmes. That's what bothers me – I can't put my hand on a motive. Here's a man dead – there's no denying that – but, so far as I can see, no reason on earth why anyone should wish him harm.

It goes without saying that Holmes comes to the rescue, and promptly solves the case.

Whereas Watson's admiration for Holmes is seemingly unbounded, the police take a somewhat different view, and lest Holmes become even more conceited than he is already, they are not averse to taking him down a peg or two by some gentle teasing if necessary. Such an opportunity arises in *The*

*Sign of Four*, when Holmes asks Inspector Athelney Jones if he remembers him from a previous encounter. The answer is not what the great detective might have hoped:

> It's Mr Sherlock Holmes, the theorist. Remember you! I'll never forget how you lectured us all on causes and inferences and effects in the Bishopgate jewel case. It's true you set us on the right track; but you'll own now that it was more by good luck than good guidance.

Likewise, in *The Red-headed League*, Mr Jones of Scotland Yard gives some advice to Mr Merryweather, a bank manager:

> You may place considerable confidence in Mr Holmes, sir. He has his own little methods, which are, if he won't mind my saying so, just a little too theoretical and fantastic, but he has the makings of a detective in him. It is not too much to say that once or twice, as in that business of the Sholto murder and the Agra treasure, he has been more nearly correct than the official force.

Finally, in *A Study in Scarlet*, Holmes admits that there are certain disadvantages in *not* being a police officer, 'Supposing I unravel the whole matter, you may be sure that [inspectors] Gregson, Lestrade and Co. will pocket all the credit. That comes of being an unofficial personage.' As for Gregson, Holmes describes him as 'the smartest of the Scotland Yarders.' Nonetheless, it is the great detective who has the last word, 'He knows that I am his superior, and acknowledges it to me; but he would cut his tongue out before he would own it to any third person.'

\* \* \*

Doyle's readers, having enjoyed to the full the exploits of Sherlock Holmes, might be forgiven for assuming the author and creator of the world's most modern, most scintillatingly brilliant, and most inexorably logical detective, shared similar qualities. A time would come, however, when certain pronouncements made by Doyle in his later life, would not only perplex his readers, but turn any such hitherto held notions, completely upside down.

6

# Doyle on a Treadmill

With the readers clamouring for the next edition of *The Strand Magazine* and its editor making Doyle offers which he could not refuse (for the Sherlock Holmes stories have now been promoted to the front pages of that publication, instead of appearing near the end), Doyle, albeit reluctantly, keeps the production line going. Not only that, but through his hero Sherlock Holmes, he dazzles his audience with the ingenuity and originality of his narratives and plots. As for the readers, they find themselves being particularly engaged with Holmes in attempting to solve the mysteries; this is because Doyle presents them with very much the same information that Holmes has at his disposal. It is like a challenge in which Doyle is asking the devotees of the great detective, 'Can you solve this for yourselves? Are you as clever as Holmes?' – to which the answer is almost invariably, 'No!'

Holmes' powers of deduction remain undimmed. Witness when, in *The Red-headed League*, he meets pawnbroker Mr Jabez Wilson for the first time and comes out with the startling conclusion, 'Beyond the obvious facts that he has at some time done manual labour, that he takes snuff, that he is a Freemason, that he has been in China, and that he has done a considerable amount of writing lately, I can deduce nothing else.' Mr Wilson duly confirms that yes, he had once performed manual labour as a ship's carpenter. But how did Holmes deduce this fact?:

> 'Your hands, my dear sir. Your right hand is quite a size larger than your left. You have worked with it, and the muscles are more developed.' "Well, the snuff, then, and the Freemasonry?" "I won't insult your

intelligence by telling you how I read that, especially as, rather against the strict rules of your order, you use an arc-and-compass breastpin.'

As for the writing:

'What else can be indicated by that right cuff so very shiny for five inches, and the left one with the smooth patch near the elbow where you rest it upon the desk?'"And finally China?"'The fish that you have tattooed immediately above your right wrist could only have been done in China. I have made a small study of tattoo marks and have even contributed to the literature of the subject. That trick of staining the fishes' scales of a delicate pink is quite peculiar to China. When, in addition, I see a Chinese coin hanging from your watch-chain, the matter becomes even more simple.'

Also in *The Red-headed League*, Holmes deduces from the appearance of the trousers of pawnbroker's assistant John Clay (alias Spaulding), that he has been digging. Says he to Watson, 'You must yourself have remarked how worn, wrinkled, and stained they were. They spoke of those hours of bur-rowing.' In fact, whilst Clay's employer Jabez Wilson had been enticed out of his shop by a ruse, the appropriately named Clay, had been busily engaged in digging a tunnel in order to gain access to a bank.

In *The Adventure of the Dancing Men*, Doyle dangles a vital clue under the very noses of his readers, as will now be seen. Mr Hilton Cubitt of Ridling Thorpe Manor, Norfolk presents Holmes with a sheet of paper on which are drawn a series of dancing men in various poses. Cubitt tells Holmes that the first dancing men were discovered written in chalk on one of the win-dow-sills of his house and that when more were found on a piece of paper left lying on the sundial in the garden, the sight of them had caused his wife to become terrified; so much so that she fainted. (In order to give his readers the same access to these so-called 'dancing men', Doyle thoughtfully draws a facsimile of them, which he duly inserts into the text of the story.) Having been shown this paper by Cubitt, Holmes becomes intrigued, saying, 'These hieroglyphics have evidently a meaning. If it is a purely arbitrary one, it may be impossible for us to solve it. If, on the other hand, it is systematic, I have no doubt that we shall get to the bottom of it.'

If he is to break the code Holmes realises that he requires a larger sample. More dancing men must be obtained before he can come to any definite opinion. Sure enough, Cubitt soon returns with further copies of dancing men which he has discovered. Holmes now meets the challenge with every atom of concentration which he can muster. Says Watson:

> For two hours I watched him as he covered sheet after sheet of paper with figures and letters, so completely absorbed in his task that he had evidently forgotten my presence. Sometimes he was making progress, and whistled and sang at his work; sometimes he was puzzled and would sit for a long spell with a furrowed brow and a vacant eye. Finally he sprang from his chair with a cry of satisfaction, and walked up and down the room rubbing his hands together.

In fact, Holmes has solved the riddle by making use of the fact that 'E' is the most common letter in the English language. The degree of frequency in which the other letters occur is more problematical, but 'speaking roughly', says Holmes, 'T' is the next most common followed by A, O, N, S, H, R, D and L. This is why he required several series-samples of the dancing men before he could ascertain their meaning.

In *A Scandal in Bohemia,* Holmes receives a letter which is both undated and unaddressed. He examines the wording of it carefully and deduces that the person who wrote it is a German, 'Do you note the peculiar construction of the sentence ... A Frenchman or Russian could not have written that. It is the German who is so uncourteous to his verbs.'

In *The Adventure of the Norwood Builder,* Holmes makes an even more astounding deduction. Inspector Lestrade is in possession of a will, the reading of which is causing him some difficulty, 'I can read the first few lines, and these in the middle of the second page, and one or two at the end. Those are as clear as print, but the writing in between is very bad, and there are three places where I cannot read it at all.' Holmes comes to the rescue by stating that he believes the document to have been written on a train, '... the good writing represents stations, the bad writing movement, and the very bad writing passing over points.'

As if this is not enough, Holmes astounds Lestrade even further by declaring that in his opinion, the will 'was drawn up on a suburban line, since nowhere, save in the immediate vicinity of a great city, could there be so quick a succession of points,' and he even goes so far as to suggest that the train in question was the express from Norwood (where builder Mr Jonas Oldacre has apparently been murdered) to London Bridge.

The criminal characters that feature in the Sherlock Holmes stories often go to great lengths and employ extraordinary tactics in order to throw the great detective off the scent. In *The Adventure of the Priory School*, Reuben Hayes, landlord of The Fighting Cock Inn, has abducted the only son of the Duke of Holdernesse from his school. Hayes committed his crime on horseback, riding across a lonely moor. But how could this be, when there were no signs of the horse's shoeprints? Only a genius of Holmes' calibre could have realised that, 'This fellow Hayes had shod his horses with shoes which counterfeited the tracks of cows.'

In the battle between criminal and detective, psychology can also play a part as in *A Scandal in Bohemia,* where Holmes uses this to his advantage. Here he is faced with the problem of discovering the whereabouts of a compromising photograph, that of two people: the beautiful Irene Adler and Wilhelm Gottsreich Sigismond von Ormstein, Grand Duke of Cassel-Felstein and hereditary King of Bohemia. The photograph was taken in the King's youth when he was Crown Prince, and he is anxious to retrieve it, in order to protect his reputation. Having made several unsuccessful attempts to this end – including having his agents burgle Irene's house – he now brings his problem to Holmes, even though he is sceptical of the chances of success: 'But how will you look?' "I will not look", replies Holmes. 'What then?' "I will get her to show me."

Sure enough, Holmes gains admittance to the sitting room of Irene's house by a ruse whereupon at a given signal, Watson throws a plumber's smoke rocket (used by members of that profession to detect leaks in pipes) into the room. Thinking that her house is on fire, Irene 'responded beautifully', leading Holmes to deduce that the photograph is kept 'in a recess behind a sliding panel just above the right bell-pull.'

As always, having feasted on his latest offering in *The Strand Magazine*, Doyle's readers are now suffering from mixed emotions. Yes, they found the story riveting and compulsive reading as always. Yes, they are in even greater awe of the great detective whilst at the same time kicking themselves for not being as clever as he is in solving the case. And, of course, they cannot wait for the next episode when they, along with Holmes, can have the chance of pitting their wits against robbers, blackmailers, murderers and the like, who for one reason or another have brought themselves to Holmes' attention.

But what of Holmes himself? What are his thoughts on the matter? When the case of *The Red-headed League* is brought to a successful conclusion, Watson offers his congratulations:

'You reasoned it out beautifully. It is so long a chain, and yet every link rings true.'

'It saved me from ennui,' he answered, yawning. 'Alas! I already feel it closing in upon me. My life is spent in one long effort to escape from the commonplaces of existence. These little problems help me to do so.'

In other words, for Holmes the exercise was worthwhile, not principally because the culprits have been apprehended and justice has been done, but because Holmes has been saved from boredom. For him, therefore, pitting his wits against criminals and solving crimes was a kind of therapy.

★   ★   ★

For Doyle, the question was how long could he continue to write his Sherlock Holmes stories when his heart was not in it. The answer is, not long, and when the parting of the ways came it came in a most dramatic manner, as will shortly be seen.

# 7

# Literary Allusions, Imagery, Music

Amongst the genre of writers of detective fiction, Doyle's prose ranks most highly (the same being true of his historical novels). An excellent example of it may be found in *The Man With the Twisted Lip*, where Watson is describing a journey from Baker Street to Lee in Kent that he is making with Holmes; the object of which being to investigate the disappearance of one of Watson's friends and his wife:

> … we dashed away through the endless succession of sombre and deserted streets, which widened gradually, until we were flying across a broad balustraded bridge, with the murky river flowing sluggishly beneath us. Beyond lay another dull wilderness of bricks and mortar, its silence broken only by the heavy, regular footfall of the policeman, or the songs and shouts of some belated party of revellers. A dull wrack was drifting slowly across the sky, and a star or two twinkled dimly here and there through the rifts of the clouds.

From time to time, in the Sherlock Holmes stories a quotation appears, indicating that their creator Doyle has an excellent literary grounding. For example, in *The Empty House*, Holmes arranges for an effigy of himself to be made and silhouetted against the window of his Baker Street apartment to decoy a would-be assassin who was planning to take a shot at him. Watson sees the effigy and cannot contain his admiration, 'Good heavens!' he cries, 'It's marvellous.' Whereupon the gratified Holmes responds by adapting a quotation from Shakespeare's *Antony and Cleopatra* to his own use, 'I trust that age doth not wither nor custom stale my infinite variety. It really is rather like me, is it not?'

Watson again congratulates Holmes for his solving of the case of *The Red-headed League*, describing him as 'a benefactor of the race.' On this occasion, Holmes responds by quoting the words of one French novelist to another: 'Well, perhaps, after all, it is of some little use,' he remarked. '*L'homme c'est rien – l'oeuvre c'est tout*, [man is nothing – art is everything] as Gustave Flaubert wrote to George Sand.'

Another hallmark of a great writer is his or her use of imagery and Doyle uses this to great effect in *The Adventure of the Norwood Builder*, when Holmes deplores the fact that 'London has become a singularly uninteresting city since the death of the late lamented Professor Moriarty.' This was not the case when Moriarty – Holmes' most famous adversary – was alive, for then that evil genius was always on Holmes' mind, 'Often it was only the smallest trace, Watson, the faintest indication, and yet it was enough to tell me that the great malignant brain was there, as the gentlest tremors of the edges of the web remind one of the foul spider which lurks in the centre.'

For Doyle's readers there is further imagery to be enjoyed in *The Sign of Four*, when Holmes declares:

How sweet the morning air is! See how that one little cloud floats like a pink feather from some gigantic flamingo. Now the red rim of the sun pushes itself over the London cloud-bank. It shines on a good many folk, but on none, I dare bet, who are on a stranger errand than you and I. How small we feel, with our petty ambitions and strivings in the presence of the great elemental forces of Nature! Are you well up in your Jean Paul? (a reference to the French existentialist philosopher, dramatist and novelist Jean-Paul Sartre.)

* * *

Music is a subject very close to Holmes' heart and one for which he has tremendous enthusiasm. In the mystery of *The Red-headed League*, Holmes:

… suddenly sprang out of his chair with the gesture of a man who has made up his mind, and put his pipe down upon the mantelpiece. 'Sarasate [Pablo – Spanish violinist and composer] plays at the St. James's Hall this afternoon,' he remarked. 'What do you think, Watson? Could your patients spare you for a few hours? There is a good deal of

German music on the programme, which is rather more to my taste than Italian or French. It is introspective, and I want to introspect.'

Again, in *A Study in Scarlet*, Holmes expresses his joy at the prospect of attending a musical concert:

And now for lunch, and then for [Wilma] Norman-Neruda [Czech violinist]. Her attack and her bowing are splendid. What's that little thing of Chopin's she plays so magnificently: Tra-la-la-lira-lira-lay.

For Holmes, listening to music was not only an excellent way of composing himself before a case but also of winding down after it. Having solved the mystery of *The Hound of the Baskervilles,* he suggests that he and Watson:

... turn our thoughts into more pleasant channels. I have a box for *Les Huguenots* [the opera by German/Jewish composer Giacomo Mayerbeer, composed in 1836]. Have you heard the De Reszkes? Might I trouble you then to be ready in half an hour, and we can stop at Marcini's for a little dinner on the way?

In *The Adventure of the Cardboard Box,* Watson describes taking a meal with Holmes, where the latter:

would talk about nothing but violins, narrating with great exultation how he had purchased his own Stradivarius, which was worth at least five hundred guineas, at a Jew broker's in Tottenham Court Road for fifty-five shillings. This led him to [Italian violinist and composer Niccolo] Paganini, and we sat for an hour over a bottle of claret while he told me anecdote after anecdote of that extraordinary man.

In *A Study in Scarlet,* Watson describes Holmes' playing of the violin which was a hobby of his, but not in the normal adulatory terms with which he was wont to idolise his hero:

... that he could play pieces, and difficult pieces, I knew well, because at my request he has played me some of Mendelssohn's *Lieder*, and other favourites. When left to himself, however, he would seldom produce any music or attempt any recognized air. Leaning back in his arm-chair of an evening, he would close his eyes and scrape carelessly at the fiddle which was thrown across his knee. Sometimes the chords were sonorous and melancholy. Occasionally they were fantastic and cheerful. Clearly they reflected the thoughts which possessed him, but whether the music aided those thoughts, or whether the playing was simply the result of a whim or fancy, was more than I could determine. I might have rebelled against these exasperating solos had it not been that he usually terminated them by playing in quick succession a whole series of my favourite airs as a slight compensation for the trial upon my patience.

Music gives Holmes the opportunity to ponder on those profound matters which touch upon the question of what it really means to be a human being. This is apparent in *A Study in Scarlet,* where Holmes and Watson attend a musical concert together, one which, when it is over, the former describes as 'magnificent':

Do you remember what Darwin [Charles Robert – English naturalist and originator with Alfred Russell Wallace of the theory of natural selection] says about music? He claims that the power of producing and appreciating it existed among the human race long before the power of speech was arrived at. Perhaps that is why we are so subtly influenced by it. There are vague memories in our souls of those misty centuries when the world was in its childhood.

This is Holmes, thinking thoughts which impinge not only on music but also on philosophy and religion. Doubtless Doyle himself often pondered what life must have been like in ancient times. His mention of 'memories' and 'the soul' brings to mind the present day science of genetics, one which would undoubtedly have been of profound interest to him, and raises the question as to whether memory and experience can be handed down through the generations by way of the genes. (The subject of genetic inheritance would later prove to be of enormous relevance when it came to the question of explaining why suddenly Doyle himself, in middle life, changed from a rational human being into a seemingly irrational one.)

Finally, it is interesting to observe how Doyle prefers to use the real-life names of those various composers and musicians whom he mentions in his texts, and perhaps from this one may deduce that he himself had a great love of the art, and that these names meant as much to him as they did to Holmes.

Although music receives scant mention in Doyle's autobiography, he came from a musical family, in that his aunts Adelaide and Annette and his uncle Frank played the pianoforte, and his uncle James played the violoncello. His own daughter Mary would one day become pianist for the Scolia Folk-song Quartette. However, it was only in the last few months of his life that Doyle himself said that he 'wanted to learn something of music'.[1]

# 8

# Dr John H. Watson

Why, it may be asked, did Doyle include the character of Dr Watson in his Sherlock Holmes stories? Was it simply that just as a great portrait painter might employ a lesser artist to execute the background of his work, so Watson was there simply to provide background material? The answer is no – there was more to it than that.

The reader cannot help but compare Watson with his less discerning mind with the brilliance of Holmes, which in consequence appears to shine even brighter; the latter not being slow to point this out. The trick is for Holmes to present Watson with a set of facts whereupon Watson comes to a conclusion, makes a hash of it and then has the error of his ways pointed out to him in no uncertain terms by Holmes. This is precisely what happens in *The Hound of the Baskervilles*, when a visitor, whom neither Holmes nor Watson has met, inadvertently leaves his walking stick at Baker Street. Invited by Holmes to examine the stick, Watson ventures an opinion which in the eyes of the former is both inadequate and erroneous. This prompts Holmes to declare loftily:

It may be that you are not yourself luminous, but you are a conductor of light. Some people without possessing genius have a remarkable power of stimulating it. I confess, my dear fellow, that I am very much in your debt.

Watson, ever loyal, ever self-effacing colludes with Holmes in running his own self down, and often to an embarrassing degree as in *The Red-headed League*, when he says:

I trust that I am not more dense than my neighbours, but I was always oppressed with a sense of my own stupidity in my dealings with Sherlock Holmes. Here I had heard what he had heard, I had seen what he had seen, and yet from his words it was evident that he saw clearly not only what had happened but what was about to happen, while to me the whole business was still confused and grotesque.

Another, and most important, reason for the presence of Watson in the stories is that as Holmes' chronicler he is a *sine qua non* as far as the reader is concerned. In other words – no Watson, no stories! It has to be said, however, that his efforts in this regard are met by Holmes with a certain lack of grace. In respect of *The Adventure of the Copper Beeches*, for instance, Holmes begins by paying both himself and Watson a compliment:

It is pleasant to me to observe, Watson, that you have so far grasped this truth that in these little records of our cases which you have been good enough to draw up, and, I am bound to say, occasionally to embellish, you have given prominence not so much to the many *causes célèbres* and sensational trials in which I have figured but rather to those incidents which may have been trivial in themselves, but which have given room for those faculties of deduction and of logical synthesis which I have made my special province.

However, it is Holmes' opinion that Watson had, '… erred perhaps in attempting to put colour and life into each of your statements instead of confining yourself to the task of placing upon record that severe reasoning from cause to effect which is really the only notable feature about the thing.'

His advice to Watson was that '… it is upon the logic rather than upon the crime that you should dwell.' Watson, having failed to do this, had therefore, 'degraded what should have been a course of lectures into a series of tales.' Holmes' opinion was that yes, Watson had avoided the mistake of being over sensational in his accounts, but in so doing, he:

…may have bordered on the trivial. … my dear fellow, what do the public, the great unobservant public, who could hardly tell a weaver by his tooth or a compositor by his left thumb, care about the finer shades of analysis and deduction!

And of course in this, Holmes is quite wrong for 'the finer shades of analysis and deduction' are precisely what they *do* care about; this being at the very core of the Holmes stories.

In *The Adventure of The Abbey Grange*, Holmes is even more scathing and *does* accuse Watson of sensationalism:

> Your fatal habit of looking at everything from the point of view of a story instead of as a scientific exercise has ruined what might have been an instructive and even classical series of demonstrations. You slur over work of the utmost finesse and delicacy in order to dwell upon sensational details which may excite but cannot possibly instruct the reader.

Even for the long-suffering Watson, this is too much. Then, 'Why do you not write them yourself?' he says irritably:

> I will, my dear Watson, I will. At present I am, as you know, fairly busy, but I propose to devote my declining years to the composition of a textbook which shall focus the whole art of detection into one volume.

This difference of opinion between Holmes and Watson may, in a sense, be construed as Doyle the physician, whose training required him to stick rigidly to the facts, holding a debate in his own mind about the nature of his writings. As 'Holmes', he sees no place for sensationalism, in what is essentially a process of scientific analysis and deduction. However, as 'Watson', he is conscious that he is writing for a wider audience and it is therefore important that, in Watson's own words, the accounts are 'novel and of interest' rather than being dry and academically worded.

One might speculate that if Doyle had continued in the medical profession instead of abandoning it for a career as a writer, then perhaps he might be remembered today as the author of a medical textbook rather than as the creator of Sherlock Holmes.

For all his criticism of Watson, Holmes is quite adept at turning on the charm when he requires his services, making no secret of the fact that he cannot really do without him. This is apparent in *A Scandal in Bohemia,* where King Wilhelm of Bohemia is anxious to discuss with Holmes a matter of some delicacy which involves Irene Adler, a woman of great beauty with whom he had had a former alliance. When Watson makes to leave,

Holmes immediately intervenes, 'Not a bit, Doctor. Stay where you are. I am lost without my Boswell.' (A reference to James Boswell, chronicler of the writer, critic and compiler of dictionaries, Dr Samuel Johnson).

Holmes, however, has no compunction about extracting Watson from his bed in the middle of the night or snatching him away from a fishing holiday if his colleague is required for a case. And although he is not slow to voice his appreciation, his remarks convey the impression that Watson's presence is to be for practical purposes only. Even if Holmes did enjoy Watson's companionship, he would never admit to it! This is borne out in *The Boscombe Valley Mystery*, where the former observes, 'It is really very good of you to come, Watson. It makes a considerable difference to me, having someone with me on whom I can thoroughly rely. Local aid is always either worthless or else biased.'

It is in *The Boscombe Valley Mystery* that Holmes suggests to Watson that they travel together to the county of Herefordshire to investigate a case, to which the ever-willing Watson agrees, observing that, 'My experience of camp life in Afghanistan had at least had the effect of making me a prompt and ready traveller.'

On occasions, Holmes' mask of inscrutability slips, and he betrays his true emotions. This occurs in *A Study in Scarlet,* where Watson, having met with Holmes for the first time, praises the detective, telling him, 'you have brought detection as near an exact science as it ever will be brought in this world.' At this, says Watson, 'My companion flushed up with pleasure at my words, and the earnest way in which I uttered them. I had already observed that he was as sensitive to flattery on the score of his art as any girl could be of her beauty.'

In the same story, Holmes takes the opportunity to acquaint Watson with his 'shortcomings' in another rare episode of introspection and frankness, 'I get in the dumps at times, and don't open my mouth for days on end. You must not think I am sulky when I do that. Just let me alone, and I'll soon be right.'

There are times when even the mighty Holmes defers to Watson for his knowledge and skill as a medical practitioner as in *The Sign of Four*, when victim Bartholomew Sholto is killed by a poisoned dart. Having examined the body, Holmes turns to Watson:

'… just put your hand here on this poor fellow's arm, and here on his leg. What do you feel?'

'The muscles are as hard as a board.'

'Quite so. They are in a state of extreme contraction, far exceeding the usual rigor mortis. Coupled with this distortion of the face, this Hippocratic smile, or *risus sardonicus* as the old writers called it, what conclusion would it suggest to your mind?'

'Death from some powerful vegetable alkaloid, some strychnine-like substance which would produce tetanus.'

As modern crime writer Val McDermid points out, the reader of a detective novel enjoys being frightened, but safely frightened, that is, within the confines of a safe environment. In *The Red-headed League*, when the two embark on a mission to trap a criminal gang, Holmes gives Watson a warning, 'I say, Doctor, there may be some little danger, so kindly put your army revolver in your pocket.' (For some reason, it is the doctor, a person whose normal duties involve the saving of lives, who is expected to carry a lethal weapon, rather than the detective Holmes, but of course, in a former life, Watson was also a soldier). Holmes also makes it clear that the gun is not simply there as a deterrent when, referring to a gang who are about to rob a bank, he instructs his colleague thus, 'When I flash a light upon them, close in swiftly. If they fire, Watson, have no compunction about shooting them down.' With Watson on hand, the reader knows that Holmes is safe, or relatively so. And if he is unfortunate enough to be injured, then who better than the good doctor to patch him up?

For all the insults and discomforts that he is obliged to endure at the hands of Holmes, poor Watson is content to live off the occasional crumbs of comfort which fall from the great detective's lips. One such crumb is thrown to him in *The Hound of the Baskervilles*, when Holmes, having asked Watson to travel alone to Dartmoor, declares that when what is to be an 'ugly' and 'dangerous' mission is finally over, 'I give you my word that I shall be very glad to have you back safe and sound in Baker Street once more.'

Finally, Watson also fulfils the important role of being the vehicle by which the stories are enabled to move forward. After all, were it not for his dialogues with Holmes, how else would the reader discover the thoughts, stratagems and exploits of the great detective?

(Incidentally, the expression, 'Elementary, my dear Watson' was not used by Doyle but by his son Adrian, in his own Sherlock Holmes story, *The Adventures of Arnsworth Castle*).

## 9

# The Demise of Holmes

To return to the real world. In January 1892, Doyle's father Charles was transferred from the Montrose Royal Asylum to the Royal Edinburgh Asylum on account of his poor mental and physical condition. Finally, in May 1892, he was admitted to the Crichton Royal [mental] Hospital, Dumfries.

In the year 1893, Doyle, exasperated by having to spend so much time on the Holmes stories when he would have much preferred to be writing in a more serious and literary vein, decides finally to do away with Sherlock Holmes. To this end, in the story *The Final Problem*, which appeared in *The Strand Magazine* in December 1893, Holmes acquaints Watson with the person whom, according to Doyle's plan, will be Holmes' nemesis:

'You have probably never heard of Professor Moriarty?'
'Never.'
'Aye, there's the genius and the wonder of the thing!' he cried. 'The man pervades London, and no one has heard of him. That's what puts him on a pinnacle in the records of crime. I tell you, Watson, in all seriousness, that if I could beat that man, if I could free society of him, I should feel that my own career had reached its summit, and I should be prepared to turn to some more placid line in life.'

Holmes then gives Watson some further details of the person with whom he is shortly to have his final and most challenging encounter. Moriarty, he says:

...is a man of good birth and excellent education, endowed by nature with a phenomenal mathematical faculty. At the age of twenty-one he wrote a treatise upon the Binomial Theorem, which has had a European vogue. On the strength of it he won the Mathematical Chair at one of our smaller universities, and had, to all appearance, a most brilliant career before him. But the man had hereditary tendencies of the most diabolical kind. A criminal strain ran in his blood, which, instead of being modified, was increased and rendered infinitely more dangerous by his extraordinary mental powers.

(Here Doyle is unwittingly anticipating the advances in the science of genetics which would take place in the following century, and provide information to indicate that yes, there may well be a genetic factor at work in the make up of a criminal.)

Through Holmes, and using his by now familiar technique, Doyle continues to elaborate on the brilliance of Moriarty, raising him to the status of a criminal without compare:

He is the Napoleon of crime, Watson. He is the organiser of half that is evil and of nearly all that is undetected in this great city. He is a genius, a philosopher, an abstract thinker. He has a brain of the first order. He sits motionless, like a spider in the centre of its web, but that web has a thousand radiations, and he knows well every quiver of each of them.

In Moriarty, even the mighty Holmes is forced to admit that he has met his match, 'You know my powers, my dear Watson, and yet at the end of three months I was forced to confess that I had at last met an antagonist who was my intellectual equal.'

Holmes endeavours to trap Moriarty, but the latter is wise to him, and pays a visit to Baker Street to warn him off. Holmes however, accepts the challenge and travels to the continent with Watson en route to the small village of Meiringen in Switzerland. On the way to the (water) Falls of Reichenbach, Moriarty's agents play a hoax on Watson in order to separate him from Holmes. When Watson realises the truth, he hurries back to the Falls only to find Holmes' alpenstock and a letter left by him which states, in respect of Moriarty: 'I am pleased to think that I shall be able to free society from any further effects of his presence, though I fear that it is at a cost which will give pain to my friends, and especially, my dear Watson, to you.'

To date, *The Adventures of Sherlock Holmes* (twelve stories) had been published in 1892 and *The Memoirs of Sherlock Holmes* (another twelve stories) would be published in 1894. The other two, which make up the twenty-six which he refers to, were *A Study in Scarlet* (1887), and *The Sign of Four* (1889). However, a measure of just how miserable Doyle had become in having to write Sherlock Holmes stories to order is revealed in the following comment:

> For a man who has no particular natural astuteness to spend his days in inventing problems and building up chains of inductive reasoning is a trying occupation. Besides, it is better not to rely too much upon the patience of the public, and when one has written twenty-six stories about one man, one feels that it is time to put it out of one's power to transgress any further.

These words may have come as something of a surprise to those of his readers who assumed that Doyle's astuteness came naturally. After all, how could he have written the stories if he did not possess this quality in abundance? In any event, Doyle now felt that he had exhausted a subject which, had he continued in it, would have produced only mediocrity. In his words, further Holmes stories 'would have been mere trash.'[1] Now, having freed himself from what to him was an intolerable burden, Doyle's life was his own and he was financially secure enough to do with it as he pleased. The direction he took, however, would appear to his readers to be completely out of character for the inventor of the world's first scientifically-minded detective. At Southsea, Doyle had dabbled in spiritualism. Now he would go one step further and become a subscriber to the *Proceedings of the Society for Psychical Research*.

\* \* \*

In 1893, when the thirty-four year old Doyle evinced an interest in psychical research, was this for purely academic reasons or could it be that he saw this as a means to resolve some problem that was on his mind? In order to answer this question it is necessary to look back at those formative events of his childhood and youth which may have influenced him.

## DEATH OF SIBLINGS

Of Doyle's eight siblings, two had died before reaching the age of three and his sister Annette had died at the young age of thirty-three. This was a trauma to his family, no doubt, but by no means an uncommon occurrence, at a time when mortality rates for both adults and children were high.

## THE TRAUMA OF A BROKEN HOME

Throughout Doyle's childhood he and his family struggled to cope with Charles Altamont, his alcoholic father, whose behaviour necessitated the boy being kept at boarding school for most of the time – even in the holidays – in order that he might be shielded from the destructive effects. Doyle may well have asked himself, was it God's will, simply fate or was there some deeper and more profound reason why this misfortune should have befallen his family and so deprived him of much of the love and companionship which he might otherwise have expected to receive from his parents and family?

What Doyle and his family went through in those dark days is paralleled by him in *The Adventure of the Cardboard Box*, which features 'an impulsive man … subject to occasional fits of hard drinking,' who in his own words, becomes 'like a madman when my temper gets loose.' The story concludes by Holmes asking solemnly:

> What is the meaning of it, Watson? What object is served by this circle of misery and violence and fear? It must tend to some end, or else our universe is ruled by chance, which is unthinkable. But what end? There is the great standing perennial problem to which human reason is as far from an answer as ever.

## DOYLE'S REJECTION OF CATHOLICISM

Doyle described how in his youth, listening to a speech by a man of the cloth, as far as he was concerned, drove home the first nail in the coffin of his Roman Catholic faith:

I remember that when, as a grown lad, I heard Father Murphy, a great fierce Irish priest, declare that there was sure damnation for everyone outside the church, I looked upon him with horror, and to that moment I trace the first rift which has grown into such a chasm between me and those who were my guides.[2]

... from my reading and from my studies, I found that the foundations not only of Roman Catholicism but of the whole Christian faith ... were so weak that my mind could not build upon them.[3] Never will I accept anything which cannot be proved to me. The evils of religion have all come from accepting things which cannot be proved.

The result was that he was driven to an agnosticism, even though this 'never for an instant degenerated into atheism.'[4]

Sherlock Holmes echoes the same sentiments when in *The Sign of Four*, he recommends to Watson the historian Winwood Reade's *Martyrdom of Man* (published in 1872). Written from a standpoint which is hostile to religion, the book is nevertheless described by Holmes as 'one of the most remarkable ever penned.'

\* \* \*

It is not suggested for a moment that Doyle, in his misfortunes, was in any way different from many others of his generation for whom life was precarious and often short and who were therefore led to question their faith. However, in the year 1893, two further events occurred which may well have brought the crisis in his mind to a head and propelled him on an urgent quest to seek answers to the questions 'What is the meaning of life?', and even 'What have I done to deserve this?'

## DOYLE'S WIFE LOUISE'S ILLNESS

In the summer of 1893, the Doyles holidayed in Switzerland where they paid a visit to the Reichenbach [water] Falls, which as already described, featured later in one of Doyle's most famous stories. Subsequently, Doyle's wife Louise developed a persistent cough and began coughing up blood (the medical term for which is haemoptysis). This would immediately have indicated to Doyle as a medical man, that she was suffering from pulmonary tuberculosis. As a consequence of this, Doyle arranged for Louise and himself to spend the winter of 1893/4 in Switzerland – this being considered the ideal place 'to take the cure', on account of the purity of its air. From now on, Louise would spend most of the remainder of her life at Davos Platz, in the small town of Davos, situated at an altitude of 5000 feet in the Swiss Alps. This town had become a venue for those suffering from 'consumption', as the disease was then called. It was here that the ever energetic Doyle learned to ski, and also created a golf course.

## DOYLE'S FATHER CHARLES'S DEATH

October 1893 brought another tragedy: Doyle's father Charles, now a patient at the Crichton Royal [mental] Hospital, Dumfries, died suddenly on the tenth of that month during an epileptic seizure.

★  ★  ★

Despite these past traumas, Doyle was generally happy during his time spent at Southsea, from 1882–1891. Said he:

> I had everything in those few years to make a man contented, save only the constant illness of my partner. And yet my soul was often troubled within me. I felt that I was born for something else, and yet I was not clear what that something might be. My mind felt out continually into the various religions of the world. I could no more get into the old ones, as commonly received, than a man could get into his boy's suit.[5]

It therefore seems reasonable to assume that Doyle's action in subscribing to the *Society for Psychic Research* was motivated, not simply by curiosity, but also by a desire to discover for himself both a set of values and beliefs by which he could live and also an occupation which he could regard as meaningful.

*Right:* 1 Doyle aged six, with his father Charles.

*Below:* 2 The Stonyhurst Cricket Club, 1873. Doyle, top right.

3 Doyle's mother, Mary Doyle, in 1891 at the age of fifty-three.

4 Dr Joseph Bell.

*Right:* 5 Louise Hawkins.

*Below:* 6 Basil Rathbone and Nigel Bruce, publicity still taken for Hollywood's production of *The Hound of the Baskervilles*.

7 Jeremy Brett, who played Sherlock Holmes in Granada Television's series, which included *The Hound of the Baskervilles*.

*Above:* 8 Holmes and Watson hailing a Hansom cab. A Sidney Paget illustration for *The Adventure of the Cardboard Box*.

*Right:* 9 The Struggle between Holmes and Moriarty at the Reichenbach Falls, by Sidney Paget. From *The Strand Magazine*, December 1893.

10 'A small square of paper fluttered down'. Watson discovers Holmes's 'final' letter to him. From *The Strand Magazine*, December 1893.

11 Doyle as Deputy Lieutenant of Surrey, 1902.

*Above:* 12 The Langham Hospital staff in 1900, preparing to leave for the Boer War. Doyle third from left.

*Right:* 13 Jean Leckie.

14 Doyle in the music room at Windlesham.

15 George Edalji.

*Above:* 16 Frances Griffiths and her Cottingley Fairies, July 1917.

*Right:* 17 Doyle with Eliza Ezra, daughter of Windlesham's gardener, carrying gramophone with which to lure the fairies.

18 The Doyle family and Harry Houdini, Atlantic City, USA in 1922.

19 Blairerno House: artist's impression by Gary Burdis.

BUSTING OUT.

20, 21, 22 'Busting out'; 'Trying to get out of quod'; 'Succeeded'; by Charles Doyle, from his *Diary*.

HURRAH!

23 Sunnyside inmates having a picnic, 6 June 1889, by Charles Doyle, from his *Diary*.

24 A picnic outing of inmates of Sunnyside, 6 June 1889, Charles Doyle, top left, with his *Diary*.

25 'The fairy cribbage table', by Charles Doyle, from his *Diary*.

26 'The fairy music stool', by Charles Doyle, from his *Diary*.

27 'Well met', by Charles Doyle, from his *Diary*.

28 Royal Edinburgh Asylum, West House.

29  Bust of Philippe Pinel.

*Above:* 30 The young Richard Doyle, in bed with his thoughts, by Richard Doyle, from his book *In Fairy Land*.

*Left:* 31 W.G. Grace bowls out Doyle, from *The Strand Magazine*.

# A Quest for Meaning:
# The Paranormal

What in Doyle's day was termed 'psychical' is today called 'paranormal': this latter word referring to phenomena 'lying outside the range of normal scientific investigations,' and including 'communication without physical links, telepathy, clairvoyance, movements of objects without known causes, and extrasensory perception (ESP).'[1] It so happens that at the time when Doyle was a young man, interest in the paranormal was at its height as psychologist John Beloff describes:

> The scientific study of the paranormal ... [which] is, historically speaking, the product of the conflict between science and religion that came to a head in Victorian England. It was then that the belief in an immaterial soul that animated the body when alive and survived its dissolution at death, which had been so central to most of the world's religions, had to contend against an increasingly self-confident scientific materialism.[2]

Christopher Evans, late Principal Scientific Officer at the National Physical Laboratory, Teddington, UK, takes matters further by describing how those seeking to find out what had become of the soul after a person's death became known as 'spiritualists':

> The great achievements of nineteenth-century science seem to be unfolding a universe of a depressingly materialistic kind, a vast and rather pointless cosmos made up of tiny billiard-balls known as atoms and with no trace of souls or spirits. But most Victorian

scientists brought up in the ethos of orthodox Christianity are expected to believe in the reality of an immortal, non-physical soul. For this reason a substantial body of them became involved in a minority religion of spiritualism, taking the line that if souls or spirits survive the death of the physical body, then these spirits must exist *somewhere* in the universe and should, in principal, be contactable. This remarkable period of science saw some of the outstanding brains of the time – the physicists Sir Oliver Lodge and Sir William Crookes; the Nobel Prize-winning biologist Charles Richet; the anthropologist Alfred Russel Wallace; and numerous others … – solemnly attempting to induce spirit forms to materialise in their laboratories.[3]

In fact, Lodge, Crookes and Wallace were all members of the *Society for Psychical Research* to which Doyle had now become a subscriber. So how could Doyle's readers – that devoted band who had caused the sales of *The Strand Magazine* almost to double, equate this action of his with him being the creator of that entirely rational man Sherlock Holmes, a person whose feet were firmly on the ground at all times (except possibly, when he was indulging his opium habit!)? Surely Doyle the writer was living his life vicariously through his fictional creation Holmes and must therefore of necessity be of the same ilk as the great detective. How, therefore, could science on the one hand and the uncertain, not to say bizarre world of psychic phenomena on the other, live together side by side? Doyle however, having set himself on this course, was not to be deflected from his study of the paranormal: a subject which, as the records indicate, he had been interested in for some considerable time.

As early as 1881, when he was aged twenty-one, Doyle had attended a lecture in Birmingham entitled *Does Death End All?* and he later admitted that this experience induced a strong degree of scepticism in him:

> I had at that time the usual contempt which the young educated man feels towards the whole subject which has been covered by the clumsy name of spiritualism. I had read of mediums being convicted of fraud, I had heard of phenomena which were opposed to every known scientific law, and I had deplored the simplicity and credulity which could deceive good, earnest people into believing that such bogus happenings were signs of intelligence outside our own existence.[4]

At the same time, he was aware that there were many eminent people, many of whom he admired, who *did* adhere to spiritualism.

Doyle's fascination with ghosts is reflected in his story *Selecting a Ghost* (1883), and again in *The Captain of the Pole-star* (1890), where the whaling ship of that name is haunted by the ghost of the captain's dead love.[5] *John Barrington Cowles* (1884), features a medical student who on his wedding night discovers that his betrothed is a werewolf!

In the early months of 1887, when he was at Southsea, Doyle and local architect Henry Ball conducted experiments in mental telepathy. For example, when the two of them sat in silence with Doyle making a sketch in a notebook and Ball seeing if he could reproduce it without actually seeing it, Doyle announced the result, 'I showed beyond any doubt whatever,' said he, 'that I could convey my thoughts without words.'[6]

A visit to a séance led Doyle in 1887, to send a letter to *Light*, the journal of the London Spiritualistic Alliance (the production of which he funded for a time out of his own pocket). This shows that by now he appears to have become more amenable in his mind to the idea of spiritualism, for the letter ends:

> Let me conclude, by exhorting any other searcher never to despair of receiving personal testimony, but to persevere through any number of failures, until at last, conviction comes to him as come it will....Above all, let every enquirer bear in mind that phenomena are only a means to an end, of no value at all themselves, and simply useful for giving us an assurance of an after-existence, for which we are to prepare by refining away our closer animal feelings and cultivating our higher, nobler impulses.[7]

As a result of a visit to Southsea in February 1889 of a Professor Milo de Meyer from Italy, Doyle became aware of the writings of Franz Anton Mesmer (eighteenth-century Austrian physician and the founder of mesmerism, who believed that there was a power which he called 'magnetism', that could be used to cure disease). Echoes of this occur in *The Parasite*, (1894) where experiments both in mesmerism and hypnosis are included.

Doyle describes a psychic experience that he had at Charmouth in Dorset in 1892 or 1893 where, inside a house which was reputed to be haunted, he heard a sound 'like some one belabouring a resounding table with a heavy cudgel': this, despite the fact that the doors and windows of the house were securely locked![8]

## LIFE GOES ON

In 1894, the doctors agreed to Doyle's wife Louise being allowed to return home to South Norwood. In September that year, Doyle embarked on a tour of the United States lecturing on British literature and on his own life and works. Meanwhile, Louise returned to Davos where Doyle joined her for Christmas. Summer 1895 found the Doyles first at Majola in the Swiss Canton of Grisons, after which they travelled to Caux near Lake Geneva; then to Rome, and finally, at the end of the year, to Egypt.

In January 1896, Doyle took Louise and his sister Lottie, who was now with them, on a voyage down Egypt's Nile river. It was hoped that this would be beneficial to Louise's health and allay the progress of the tuberculosis from which she was suffering. This experience inspired Doyle to write *The Tragedy of Korosko,* 1898 (about a band of travellers caught up in a Muslim revolt in the Sudan).

Sudan had been under Egyptian control since 1820 but following a revolution the country's capital Khartoum fell to Mohammed Ahmed – the Mahdi – in 1885. When Doyle heard that the Egyptian army, with British soldier and statesman Sir Herbert (later Lord) Kitchener as its commander-in-chief, was marching to re-conquer the Sudan, he arranged for himself to be appointed honorary correspondent to London's *Westminster Gazette*. However, he failed to see any real action as Kitchener's preparations were not yet complete. The Doyles returned to England in late April, 1896.

In January 1897, the family moved from South Norwood to temporary accommodation in Surrey where the air was considered to be of a better quality and therefore more conducive to Louise's health than London. By October, the family was in residence in their new house 'Undershaw' at Hindhead. Here, true to form, Doyle founded a football club, played cricket and took up riding.[9]

On 15 March 1897, Doyle met and fell in love with Jean Leckie who was the daughter of wealthy Scottish parents and currently living in Blackheath. At the time she was aged thirty-four and he was thirty-seven. However, for Doyle there was no question of divorcing Louise or of him being unfaithful to her. The following year Doyle travelled to Italy with his brother-in-law, the novelist E.W. 'Willie' Hornung (creator of the fictitious gentleman burglar 'Raffles').

In December 1899, Doyle applied to join the army to fight against the Boers but was rejected because of his age. However, when his friend John

Langman announced that he was financing a fifty-bed front line hospital for the troops in South Africa, Doyle accepted a post on its medical staff where he would fulfil the role of army doctor. To this end, on 28 February 1900, he set sail from Tilbury for Cape Town. However, on his arrival at Bloemfontein in the Orange Free State, where the Langman Hospital was established, he was not preoccupied mainly with casualties but with an epidemic of 'enteric' (typhoid) fever which 'cost us 5,000 lives'.[10]

On 5 June 1900, Pretoria, the capital of the Transvaal province, was captured by the British and it was generally assumed that the war would soon be over. In fact, it dragged on for almost another two years. Doyle, therefore, sailed from Cape Town on 11 July, on the return journey home. By now, in addition to his medical duties he had also managed to write a considerable portion of his history of the conflict.

In 1900 Doyle stood as Liberal Unionist Party parliamentary candidate for Central Edinburgh in the forthcoming general election. This party was anxious, with the ruling Conservatives, to continue the prosecution of The Boer War. He was somewhat uncertain of his motivation for becoming an MP. Said he, 'It certainly was from no burning desire to join that august assembly … [i.e. the House of Commons]. Deep in my bones I felt that I was on earth for some big purpose, and it was only by trying that I could tell that the purpose was not political.'[11] Nonetheless, having set his hand to the plough he flung himself into the campaign with typical enthusiasm. 'I was fresh from the scene of war and overflowing with zeal to help the army, so I spared myself in no way.' After a smear campaign in which Doyle was called a 'papist conspirator', 'a Jesuit emissary', and 'a Subverter of the Protestant Faith,' (which was ironic, as he had long since abandoned his belief in Roman Catholicism), he duly lost the election held in October 1900, by 569 votes. Doyle was defeated again when he stood for Parliament for a Scottish Border constituency in 1906.

On 24 October 1902, a knighthood was conferred on Doyle by King Edward VII. In the same year he was appointed Deputy-Lieutenant of Surrey.

★   ★   ★

Books published at about this time included: *The Great Boer War*, 1900 (a 500-page volume) and *The War in South Africa: its Cause and Conduct*, 1902 (a pamphlet).

# Holmes is Reborn

After Holmes' disappearance and presumed death at the Reichenbach Falls in 1891, at the hands of the evil Professor Moriarty, his friend Watson despairs of ever seeing him again. Nevertheless, his former friendship with the great detective left a lasting impression. Says Watson:

> It can be imagined that my close intimacy with Sherlock Holmes had interested me deeply in crime, and that after his disappearance I never failed to read with care the various problems which came before the public, and I even attempted more than once for my own private satisfaction to employ his methods in their solution, though with indifferent success.

Then suddenly, in 1894, Holmes reappears, and Watson is dumbfounded:

> I moved my head to look at the cabinet behind me. When I turned again Sherlock Holmes was standing smiling at me across my study table. I rose to my feet, stared at him for some seconds in utter amazement, and then it appears that I must have fainted for the first and the last time in my life. Certainly a grey mist swirled before my eyes, and when it cleared I found my collar ends undone and the tingling aftertaste of brandy upon my lips. Holmes was bending over my chair, his flask in his hand.

From the conversation that ensues however, it is clear that Watson is far more emotional about the reunion than Holmes:

'My dear Watson,' said the well-remembered voice, 'I owe you a thousand apologies. I had no idea that you would be so affected … I have given you a serious shock by my unnecessarily dramatic reappearance.' [In fact, when Holmes reappeared, it was in the disguise of an elderly and deformed man]. I gripped him by the arm.

'Holmes!" I cried. 'Is it really you? Can it indeed be that you are alive? Is it possible that you succeeded in climbing out of that awful abyss?'

Holmes' housekeeper Mrs Hudson is equally surprised by the sudden reappearance of her employer at Baker Street, and she flies into 'violent hysterics.' Holmes then goes on to describe how he and Moriarty grappled with one another on the brink of the Reichenbach Falls:

It was not a pleasant business, Watson. The fall roared beneath me. I am not a fanciful person, but I give you my word that I seemed to hear Moriarty's voice screaming at me out of the abyss. A mistake would have been fatal. More than once, as tufts of grass came out in my hand or my foot slipped in the wet notches of the rock, I thought that I was gone. But I struggled upwards, and at last I reached a ledge several feet deep and covered with soft green moss, where I could lie unseen in the most perfect comfort.

Even here, Holmes is not safe, for now it is an accomplice of the Professor who tries to kill him, 'A huge rock, falling from above, boomed past me, struck the path, and bounded over into the chasm. For an instant I thought that it was an accident; but a moment later, looking up, I saw a man's head against the darkening sky.' This leaves Holmes with no choice but to hide and remain incognito, to which end he travels to Tibet, Persia and the Sudan. Finally, having returned as far as France, he learns about the mysterious murder of the Honourable Ronald Adair in London's Park Lane by person or persons unknown. The temptation is too great, and in order to have the opportunity to investigate it for himself, he decides to return to England. 'Work is the best antidote to sorrow, my dear Watson,' said he, 'and I have a piece of work for us both tonight, which, if we can bring it to a successful conclusion, will in itself justify a man's life on this planet.' The two of them would now embark on a stratagem to solve what would become known as *The Adventure of The Empty House*.

\* \* \*

Although *The Adventure of the Empty House* was published in 1903, Holmes and Watson reappear prior to this date in *The Hound of the Baskervilles*, which was serialised in *The Strand* in 1901. It is made clear however, that at this point Holmes has not come alive again. This is simply an untold story from the past. It is a huge success, which quickly becoems a best-seller when subsequently published in book form. This prompts the American magazine *Collier's Weekly* to offer Doyle the sum of $45,000 for thirteen more stories, and the editor Greenhough Smith of *The Strand* to offer a further £100 per thousand words on top of this. For Doyle, the temptation is too great and as much as he would prefer to occupy himself in other ways, he agrees to oblige.

★   ★   ★

According to Dr Watson *The Adventure of the Abbey Grange* (published in 1905) was intended:

> to be the last of those exploits of my friend Mr. Sherlock Holmes, which I should ever communicate to the public. This resolution of mine was not due to any lack of material, since I had notes of many hundreds of cases to which I have never alluded, nor was it caused by any waning interest on the part of my readers in the singular personality and unique methods of this remarkable man. The real reason lay in the reluctance which Mr Holmes has shown to the continued publication of his experiences. So long as he was in actual professional practice the records of his successes were of some practical value to him; but since he has definitely retired from London and betaken himself to study and bee farming on the Sussex Downs, notoriety has become hateful to him, and he has peremptorily requested that his wishes in this matter should be strictly observed.

However, Watson prevails upon the great detective to permit just one more of his (Watson's) chronicles to be published, *The Adventure of the Second Stain* arguing that, 'it was only appropriate that this long series of episodes should culminate in the most important international case which he has ever been called upon to handle...' In this chronicle Holmes is asked to retrieve a missing document accusing Britain of committing atrocities in South Africa, which might result in a European war if its contents were to leak out. Even this was not to be Holmes' final appearance, for he would resurface once again during the forthcoming First World War.

In 1903, Holmes retires to Sussex where he keeps bees and makes a study of their habits.

## CHIVALRY

Doyle's son Adrian presents a picture of his father as the child from a family that still held to the values and traditions of its forebears, even though it had, for the time being, come down in the world. He describes Doyle as 'living from his tenderest years in the chivalric sciences of the fifteenth century in the bosom of a family to whom pride of lineage was of infinitely greater importance than the discomforts of that comparative poverty that had come to surround them.' Doyle lived under a rigid code in which he:

> would adhere absolutely to the mediaeval values in all the basic pillars of life – women, money, courtesy to those of lower degree, pride of blood that is the condemnation of snobbery, the steel self-sacrifice that should be the natural choice of the gentleman towards his fellow way-farers – these were the codes that composed the essence my father... His belief in them gives meaning to such instances as that of my huge father, standing in his stocking feet on the gravel drive, benignly watching the departure of an old and very dirty tramp shod in his best golf shoes, and his comment – 'he needs them more than I.'[1]

Said Adrian:

> I held certain sides of him in the greatest awe. It was not a case of physical fear, but recognition of the fact that basic to the 'big-hearted, big-bodied, big-souled' [a quotation from author Jerome K. Jerome], there was the iron will that could neither understand nor forgive any deviation from the singular code that was his own.[2]

## KINDNESS AND GENEROSITY

By all accounts, Doyle gave generously to his family, having achieved success as an author. His affection also extended to his dog Carlo (a name which he also gave to the spaniel which features in *The Sussex Vampire*). When Carlo died in July 1921, Doyle wrote a poem about him describing those qualities which he most admired:

> No truer, kinder soul
> Was ever sped than thine.
> You lived without a growl,
> You died without a whine.[3]

Doyle's account of the First World War, *The British Campaign in France and Flanders*, was published on a non-profit making basis 'in order that the poorest soldier could possess an accurate account of what had been achieved through his own courage.' He also refused, 'all profits from his books on the Boer War and Great War [Second World War], his defence of [Oscar] Slater or the Congo natives [where he declined to accept any payment of royalties for his book on the subject], for his record-breaking world lecture tours on Spiritualism, and even to accept pay for his military service.'[4]

## A Man Ahead of his Time

Doyle's abhorrence of slavery and of the exploitation of indigenous peoples by colonial powers has already been mentioned. Other avant-garde subjects dealt with in his books are: alcoholism (*The Japanned Box*) and homosexuality and transvestitism (*The Man with the Watches*). In *The Five Orange Pips* (1891) and *The Yellow Face* (1893), Doyle expresses sympathy for inter-racial marriage.

★ ★ ★

In 1905, Doyle became president of the newly-created Hindhead Golf Club. In the general election of January 1906, Doyle stood once again for Parliament: this time as prospective member for the Scottish constituency of the Border Burghs. Once again, he was narrowly defeated.

On 4 July 1906, his wife Louise died from the effects of chronic tuberculosis. She was forty-nine. Over Louise's grave in Grayshott churchyard near Hindhead, Doyle erected a marble cross with an inscription which includes the following words, 'Erected by her sorrowing husband Arthur Conan Doyle, Of such is that of Heaven.' Both the cross and the word 'Heaven' have

Christian connotations, which was appropriate as his late wife had been a devout Protestant. Soon however, Doyle himself would publicly announce his adoption of an entirely different religion, as will shortly be seen.

In 1907, Doyle re-married: his new wife being Jean Leckie, 'the younger daughter of a Blackheath [Surrey] family whom I had known for years, and who was a dear friend of my mother and sister.'[5] Said to have 'an intensely dramatic nature', Jean had studied music at Dresden and Florence.[6] The couple bought a house called Little Windlesham (subsequently known simply as Windlesham), in the town of Crowborough in Sussex near to where Jean's parents had a holiday cottage. Doyle and his new wife went on to have three children: Denis, Adrian and Jean.

In the autumn of 1911, following in his father's footsteps, Doyle's son Kingsley enrolled as a medical student at St Mary's Hospital, Paddington.

★  ★  ★

Books published at around this time included *Sir Nigel*, 1906 (set at the time of The Hundred Years War) and *Through the Magic Door*, 1907. This was an appreciation by Doyle of his favourite literary figures such as Sir Walter Scott (Scottish novelist and poet), Thomas Macaulay (English writer and politician), Thomas Carlyle (Scottish historian and essayist), James Boswell (Scottish writer, and chronicler of Dr Samuel Johnson), Robert Louis Stevenson (Scottish writer), Herman Melville (US novelist, short-story writer, and poet), and Jean Froissart (French chronicler and poet). Also published was *The Lost World*, 1912 (where Professor George Challenger heads an expedition to the Amazon basin, where it is alleged that prehistoric animals have survived).

## 12

# Justice and Fair Play

Just as Doyle had made his voice known on the subject of oppression from an early age, in particular that of the native Congolese by their Belgian colonisers, so it could be argued that the entire *raison d'être* of his alter ego Sherlock Holmes was to bring criminals to justice and to correct such wrongs in society as the false conviction and imprisonment of the innocent.

*The Boscombe Valley Mystery* reflects Doyle's view that justice should always be tempered with mercy and understanding. John Turner is a murderer with whom Holmes has certain sympathy by virtue of the fact that he was being blackmailed by his victim. For this reason, the great detective agrees to keep his crime a secret for once, telling Turner, 'Well, it is not for me to judge you … .' And then, alluding to the fact that this old and sick man is soon to meet his maker, 'You are yourself aware that you will soon have to answer for your deed at a higher court than the Assizes.' This passage also indicates that although Doyle had apparently discarded his Catholic faith, nevertheless he still appears to believe in the equivalent of the Biblical Day of Judgment.

Holmes again takes the law into his own hands in *The Adventure of The Abbey Grange*, where Captain Jack Crocker fatally injures Sir Eustace Brackenstall, husband of the woman with whom the captain has always been in love – Mary. It is Holmes' opinion that the captain acted in self-defence and therefore, instead of revealing what he knows to the police, he decides to hold an impromptu mock trial:

> See here, Captain Croker, we'll do this in due form of law. You are the prisoner. Watson, you are a British jury, and I never met a man who was

more eminently fitted to represent one. I am the judge. Now, gentlemen of the jury, you have heard the evidence. Do you find the prisoner
guilty or not guilty?

Watson duly declares the prisoner to be not guilty, whereupon Holmes
continues:

*Vox populi, vox Dei* [The voice of the people is the voice of God]. You
are acquitted, Captain Croker. So long as the law does not find some
other victim, you are safe from me. Come back to this lady in a year,
and may her future and yours justify us in the judgment which we have
pronounced this night.

★   ★   ★

In the year 1903, Doyle was to prove that he was every bit as good at solving
real life criminal cases as his ace detective Sherlock Holmes was at solving
fictional ones. (In fact, Dr Joseph Bell, Doyle's old tutor at Edinburgh had
done a very similar thing when he became involved in the real life case of
Eugene Chantrelle, a Frenchman who murdered his wife). Now Doyle, to
his credit, would seize the opportunity to go beyond mere pen-pushing to
achieve his ends.

On 2 February 1903, a horse was found mutilated near the village of Great Wyrley in Staffordshire and other mutilations of both
horses and cattle were to follow. The police suspected George Edalji, a
thirty-year old solicitor who lived with his parents: his father being the
Reverend Shapurji Edalji, a Parsee Indian (one of Persian origin) who
had married an English lady and was now a member of the Church of
England.

Some years earlier, the Edalji family had received several threatening
letters which the police believed had been sent by George himself. Now,
following the mutilations, he was duly arrested, tried, convicted and sentenced to seven years hard labour. However, following a great deal of protest
– including a 10,000 signature petition delivered to the Home Office – he
was released after having served only three years in October 1906. It was
then that Doyle began to take an interest in the case. 'I realized that I was in
the presence of an appalling tragedy, and that I was called upon what I could
do to set it right.'[1]

As soon as Doyle set eyes on Edalji in a London hotel where the two had arranged to meet, he realised that it was extremely unlikely that he had committed the crime. This was because of the manner in which the convicted man was reading the newspaper:

> He held the paper close to his eyes and rather sideways, proving not only a high degree of myopia, but marked astigmatism. The idea of such a man scouring fields at night and assaulting cattle, whilst avoiding the watching police, was ludicrous to anyone who can imagine what the world looks like to eyes with myopia of 8 dioptres.[2]

Doyle published his findings in January 1907 in the form of a pamphlet entitled *The Story of Mr George Edalji*. His conclusion was that there was nothing in the evidence to indicate that Edalji 'had anything to do, either directly or indirectly, with the outrages or with the anonymous letters.'[3]

Following an investigation of the case by the Home Secretary, a government commission declared that Edalji was innocent of the attacks on the horses and cattle but guilty of writing threatening letters. He was therefore pardoned but not compensated in any way. As for Doyle, he had his own ideas about who the animal mutilator was: namely, Royden Sharpe who had been a fellow pupil with Edalji at grammar school and later worked for a butcher. This occupation would have given him access to a knife suitable for his purpose of mutilation. Significantly, Sharpe had been 'absent at sea', working on a cattle transporting ship from 1895 until 1903 when he returned home and the attacks on the animals began. Despite Doyle's monumental efforts, the Home Office refused to pursue the case he had built up against Sharpe.

* * *

Another real-life case came to Doyle's notice in 1908: the murder of an elderly spinster Marion Gilchrist of Glasgow, who was found bludgeoned to death in her parlour by her paid companion Miss Helen Lambie. Miss Gilchrist's room was in disarray and someone had clearly been rummaging through her personal papers. The only item missing from her jewellery was a diamond brooch.

When the local police discovered that a German-Jewish immigrant named Oscar Slater had recently pawned a brooch, they immediately suspected him of the crime. But before he could be arrested Slater had fled the country aboard the liner *Lusitania* under an assumed name. He was arrested when the liner docked at New York but before extradition proceedings could be implemented, Slater offered to return to Britain voluntarily in order to prove his innocence.

Despite the fact that the brooch that Slater had pawned did not match the description of the one stolen from Miss Gilchrist's house, Slater was found guilty of murder and sentenced to death. This time, a petition of 20,000 signatures was presented to the Home Office, whereupon Slater's sentence was commuted to 'life imprisonment'.

Doyle, who had already been approached by Slater's lawyers, was scornful of the prosecution's view that, 'the frail hammer' found in Slater's box of tools could have been used to inflict such severe wounds as the victim's body displayed.[4] He was also puzzled by the fact that the first doctor to attend the scene of the crime was not called upon to testify; that a chair in the victim's parlour had been wiped clean of blood and brain material (i.e. Miss Gilchrist's) before the police's forensic team arrived; that if the man whom Miss Lambie had admitted to Miss Gilchrist's home shortly before the murder was Slater – who to her was a stranger – then why did she not at once inform her mistress? In other words, Doyle felt sure that Miss Lambie had recognised the man and so could not have been Slater. Doyle, therefore, took the view that, 'this unhappy man [i.e. Slater] had, in all probability, no more to do with the murder for which he had been condemned, than I had.'[5]

Ever a one to put pen to paper in a just cause, Doyle duly published *The Case of Oscar Slater* in the summer of 1912 – in which he set out the results of his investigation. One of the points made by Doyle was that Slater had travelled abroad under a false name (with his young mistress), for no other reason than that he was still married and wished to avoid being discovered by his wife. All efforts were in vain however, for despite questions being asked in the House of Commons and an appeal being made to the Secretary of State for Scotland, there was no offer to reopen the case.

John French, a Glasgow police detective who had interviewed Lambie during the original murder enquiry, subsequently declared that on the night of the murder she had told him that the man she saw fleeing from Miss Gilchrist's flat was not Oscar Slater but Miss Gilchrist's nephew Francis Charteris, who was currently a professor at St Andrew's University.

By February 1925, Slater had served a total of sixteen years in Peterhead Prison: a fact which troubled Doyle deeply. 'From time to time one hears word of poor Slater from behind his prison walls, like the wail of some wayfarer who has fallen into a pit and implored aid from the passers-by.'[6] In 1925, Slater appealed directly to Doyle by persuading a fellow-prisoner to smuggle a note to him.

In July 1927, Glasgow journalist William Park (whom Doyle had assisted in his researches), openly suggested in his book *The Truth about Oscar Slater*, that Charteris had visited Miss Gilchrist on the night of the murder. Following further statements by Miss Lambie and by one of the original trial witnesses it appeared that there had been a cover up and that Slater had in fact been framed by the police. Finally, as a result of further publicity in newspapers such as the *Empire News* and *The Daily News*, the Secretary of State for Scotland decided that Slater should be released – an event which duly occurred on 14 November 1927. Doyle now made his innermost feelings known to Slater, 'This is to say in my wife's name and my own, how grieved we have been at the infamous justice which you have suffered at the hands of our officials.'[7] The case was re-opened, the original verdict was dismissed on a technicality and the court awarded Slater £6,000 in ex-gratia compensation. However, although Slater's conviction was quashed, the court did not go so far as to declare him innocent. It would be another fifty years or so before the full truth became known.

In the late 1980s the Slater case files were opened to the public. In them, former Special Branch Officer Thomas Toughill discovered an anonymous letter sent to the Secretary of State for Scotland the day before Slater was due to hang, accusing not Charteris but another man of the murder. This was Wingate Birrell (who, like Charteris, was also a nephew of Miss Gilchrist), and who happened to be engaged to Lambie. Birrell had also visited Miss Gilchrist on the evening of her death and it appears that the two nephews were working in cahoots, with the connivance of Lambie who had admitted them to the house. While Charteris rummaged through the elderly lady's papers, Birrell's task was to distract her.

The reason for the visit of the two nephews was connected with the fact that shortly before her death Miss Gilchrist had changed her will, leaving the bulk of her estate to her, allegedly, illegitimate daughter. It is therefore believed, that Charteris may have been searching through the papers in order to find some evidence which would make his aunt's new will invalid. However, the plan went dreadfully wrong when Birrell apparently lost his nerve and instead of simply distracting the elderly lady, battered her to death.

Doyle, who had procured the release of an innocent man from prison, did not live to see the real culprits identified. As for Birrell and his accomplice Charteris, they also died before the evidence of their guilt was forthcoming.[8]

## 13

# War, Spiritualism

With the outbreak of war in August 1914, Doyle again attempted to enlist in the army, but once again his application was rejected on the grounds that he was now aged fifty-five. Undeterred, he set about organising a local volunteer force at Crowborough for the purposes of civil defence. This prompted the War Office to authorise the establishment of volunteer regiments throughout the country, of which the Crowborough Company of the 6th Royal Sussex Volunteer Regiment was the first.[1] A plethora of suggestions was sent by Doyle to the War Office suggesting such innovations as the provision of inflatable rubber life-belts for sailors in naval ships and for the issuing of body armour to the soldiers in the front line. His pamphlets *To Arms!* and *The World War Conspiracy* extolled the virtues of the British cause.

The advent of war had a salutary effect. Said Doyle:

> … when the War came it brought earnestness into all our souls and made us look more closely at our own beliefs and reassess their values. In the presence of an agonized world, hearing every day of the deaths of the flower of our race in the first promise of their unsullied youth, seeing around one the wives and mothers who had no clear conception whither their loved one had gone to, I seemed suddenly to see that this subject with which I had so long dallied was not merely a study of a force outside the rules of science, but that it was really something tremendous, a breaking down of the walls between two worlds, a direct undeniable message from beyond, a call of hope and of guidance to the human race at the time of its deepest affliction.[2]

The war was to take a heavy toll on Doyle's family. Within three weeks of its outbreak Jean's brother Malcolm who was serving as a military doctor, was killed at Mons. On 15 July 1915, Connie and Willie Hornung's son Oscar was killed in action at Ypres. On 28 July, Lottie's husband Captain Leslie Oldham of the Royal Engineers was also killed in the trenches. Having been wounded on the Somme River battlefield in 1916 and invalided out of the army, Kingsley (Doyle's only son by his first marriage), recommenced his studies as a medical student at St Mary's Hospital Paddington.

In May 1916, Doyle visited the Western Front where he met with his brother Innes, Assistant Adjutant-General of the 24th Division, and also with his son Kingsley who had interrupted his studies at St Mary's Hospital Medical School to become Acting Captain and Medical Officer with the First Hampshire Regiment. Following this, Doyle travelled on to Italy to inspect that country's forward military positions. 1917 found Doyle once more in France, where he again visited Innes, who by this time was Assistant Adjutant-General with the British III Corps.[3]

The First World War provided Doyle with another opportunity to come to the aid of a person whom he considered to be the victim of unfair treatment: in this case, Sir Roger Casement. He and Doyle were old friends; Casement's knighthood having been given to him on account of the efforts he had made to improve the conditions of rubber workers in the Belgian Congo and in Peru; the subject of colonial oppression being one which was also very close to Doyle's own heart. However on 26 June 1916, Casement, Irish patriot and British consular official, was tried for treason at London's Old Bailey.

Casement's plight came about thus. In 1913 he became a member of the provisional committee established to act as the governing body of the Irish Volunteer Force, dedicated to the cause of Irish home rule. At the outbreak of the First World War he travelled to Berlin in order to enlist German help for Irish independence. (Here, Doyle differed from Casement in that the former was a strong advocate of the Empire.) Said Doyle, referring to Casement after the latter's arrival in Berlin:, 'He was a man of fine character, and that he should, [when] in the full possession of his senses, act as a traitor to the Country which had employed and honoured him, is inconceivable to anyone who knew him … '[4]

Doyle now petitioned the Prime Minister for Casement's life to be spared, arguing that some allowance be made for the accused man's abnormal physical and mental state. (Casement allegedly suffered from chronic headaches). In other words, it was Doyle's view that Casement, whom he regarded as a traitor, had taken leave of his senses. Doyle's efforts were to no avail and Casement was hanged at Pentonville Prison on 3 August 1916.

★   ★   ★

As a young man Doyle once said, 'Never will I accept anything which cannot be proved to me. The evils of religion have all come from accepting things which cannot be proved.'[5] Now, this statement was but a distant memory for him because as time went by he became more and more convinced of the truth of spiritualism, despite the warnings of those who were more sceptical of it and urged caution. They included Jerome K. Jerome (English humorous writer, novelist and playwright); Frank Podmore (psychic researcher); J.M. Barrie (Scottish novelist and dramatist); H.G. Wells (English novelist, short-story writer and popular historian); George Bernard Shaw (Irish dramatist and critic).

Although in a 1917 edition of *The Strand Magazine* Doyle made it clear how well aware he was of the pitfalls which lay in wait for the unwary researcher into spiritualism, equally he believed he had avoided them and thereby reaped his reward:

It is treacherous and difficult ground, where fraud lurks and self-deception is possible and falsehood from the other side is not unknown. There are setbacks and disappointments for every investigator. But if one picks one's path one can win through and reach the reward beyond – a reward which includes great spiritual peace, an absence of fear in death, and an abiding consolation in the death of those whom we love. It is, I repeat, this religious teaching which is the great gift that has been granted in our time.[6]

Doyle now felt confident enough of his new-found religion to make his feelings known to the world. Addressing the London Spiritualist Alliance on 25 October 1917, he referred to an 'interesting spiritual experience which had occurred to me in a séance.' His interest in the subject [of spiritualism], he said, was 'one of some standing, and I may fairly claim since it is only within the last year or so that I have finally announced that I was satisfied with the evidence, that I have not been hasty in forming my opinion.' For Doyle therefore, the messages were authentic and it was now time to accept this and embrace their meaning. Said he:

When an inquirer has convinced himself of the truth of the phenomena, there is no real need to pursue the matter further. The real object of the investigation is to give us assurance in the future and spiritual strength in the present, to give us a clear perception of the fleeting nature of matter and reveal the eternal values beyond all the shows of time and sense – the things which are indeed lasting, going on and ever on through the ages in a glorious and majestic progression.[8]

Doyle justified his belief in spiritual revelation by the following rhetorical argument:

People ask me, not unnaturally, what is it which makes me so perfectly certain that this thing is true. That I am perfectly certain is surely demonstrated by the mere fact that I have abandoned my congenial and lucrative work, left my home for long periods at a time, and subjected myself to all sorts of inconveniences, losses, and even insults, in order to get the facts home to the people... I may say briefly that there is no physical sense which I possess which has not been separately assured... I have seen my mother and my nephew, young Oscar Hornung [offspring of his sister Connie and her husband the novelist Willie Hornung], as plainly as I ever saw them in life – so plainly that I could almost have counted the wrinkles of the one and the freckles of the other ... All fine-drawn theories of the subconscious go to pieces before the plain statement of the intelligence, 'I am a spirit. I am Innes. I am your brother.'[9]

From now on:

The objective side of it [spiritualism] ceased to interest, for having made up one's mind that it was true there was an end of the matter. The religious side of it was clearly of infinitely greater importance. The telephone bell is in itself a very childish affair, but it may be the signal for a very vital message.[10]

In November 1917, in the magazine *Light* he elaborated on his views of the 'spiritual body' (he omitted to use the word soul), which to his way of thinking was unchanging (immortal):

Death makes no abrupt change in the process of development, nor does it make an impassable chasm between those who are on either side of it. No trait of the form and no peculiarity of the mind are changed by death but all are continued in that spiritual body which is the counterpart of the earthly one at its best, and still contains within it that core of spirit which is the very essence of the man.[11]

(In this, Doyle was reflecting the ideas of the spiritualist Major Alfred Drayson, his former acquaintance from Portsmouth.)

Through writings and lecture tours, Doyle would now make the whole world aware of the fact that he had embraced spiritualism, a means by which he was able to be in regular contact with his deceased relatives and friends. Soon he would take this one step further and surprise – not to say shock – his followers even more!

\* \* \*

Under pressure from the 'Premier' of wartime Britain, Sherlock Holmes comes out of retirement one last time in *His Last Bow*, where he lends his support to the countering of German espionage. Subtitled *The War Service of Sherlock Holmes*, the story was published in 1917 in *The Strand Magazine*; on the cover of which appeared the words, 'Sherlock Holmes outwits a German spy.' Says Holmes:

There's an east wind coming, Watson, such a wind as never blew on England yet. It will be cold and bitter… and a good many of us may wither before its blast. But it's God's own wind none the less, and a cleaner, better, stronger land will lie in the sunshine when the storm has cleared.

How prophetic these words had proved to be, bearing in mind the tremendous loss of life which occurred in the trenches of the First World War. Holmes finally dies in obscurity, the cause and place of his death and the location of his grave remaining forever unknown.

As far as Sherlock Holmes was concerned Doyle's legacy was to give deep and enduring pleasure to his millions of admirers throughout the world. Not only that, but certain police forces were quick to learn from Holmes' thorough and innovative investigatory techniques. His son Adrian mentioning, for example: 'The training of the Egyptian police upon his methods, the significant gesture of the French sûreté in naming the great Lyons crime laboratories in honour of Conan Doyle, and the tribute of the Police College of China ... '[12]

\* \* \*

In 1918 the Australian High Command invited Doyle to inspect Anzac positions on the Somme River where he came under artillery fire and saw the death and mutilation of both soldiers and animals at first hand. These experiences led to his publication of *The British Campaign in France and Flanders* (in six volumes). Meanwhile, on a lighter note, he produced *The Valley of Fear* (serialised 1914–15), a Sherlock Holmes story set largely in Pennsylvania, USA.

Having survived the war, Kingsley died on 28 October 1918 in the pan-European influenza epidemic. On the eleventh of the following month, hostilities ended with the signing of the Armistice. However, now another tragedy came for Doyle and his family when, on 19 February 1919, his brother Innes, who had also survived the war, perished in the same influenza epidemic that had killed Kingsley.

# Fairies

Doyle was now a confirmed spiritualist: someone who believed in psychic phenomena and who was regularly in contact with the spirits of his deceased family and friends. Now he was to announce his belief in something even more bizarre.

Given the fact that Doyle's parents were both descended from Irish stock, it is not surprising that fairies featured in their backgrounds to some extent. In fact, Doyle's son Adrian confirms that as a child his father interpreted the works of Jean Froissart (fourteenth-century French chronicler and poet) and Enguarrand de Monstrelet (fifteenth-century French chronicler) as fairy stories.[1]

However much a child may believe in fairy stories, the normal course of events is for him or her to grow out of such beliefs before the attainment of adulthood. Not so with Doyle. In 1922, having investigated an event which had occurred five years earlier, sixty-three year old Doyle suddenly made the astonishing announcement that he actually believed in fairies!

This professed belief of Doyle's, which he made no secret of, came as yet another surprise to his readers and acquaintances even though many of them were doubtless aware of the traditional association between fairies and the Irish. According to a recent article posted on the internet there are 'good historical explanations' for the existence of the 'little people' of Irish legend. They recount:

> …many and frequent invasions where the intruders force the invaders underground to forever dwell beneath earth and mound. Many of these dispossessed natives were said to possess the supernatural powers, which either remained benign, or were contorted by bitterness into mischief.

The fairies and spirits became nocturnal creatures to avoid discovery by the raiders, who believed they had slaughtered all of them.

Despite this, the fairies were, 'occasionally malicious, but rarely, if ever, malevolent.'[2]

Doyle's book *The Coming of the Fairies*, published in 1922, begins with the following extraordinary statement:

The series of incidents set forth in this little volume represent either the most elaborate and ingenious hoax ever played upon the public, or else they constitute an event in human history which may in the future appear to have been epoch-making in its character. It is hard for the mind to grasp what the ultimate results may be if we have actually proved the existence upon the surface of this planet of a population which may be as numerous as the human race, which pursues its own strange life in its own strange way, and which is only separated from ourselves by some difference of vibrations. We see objects within the limits which make up our colour spectrum, with infinite vibrations, unused by us, on either side of them. If we could conceive a race of beings which were constructed in material which threw out shorter or longer vibrations, they would be invisible unless we could tune ourselves up or tone them down. It is exactly that power of tuning up and adapting itself to other vibrations which constitutes a clairvoyant, and there is nothing scientifically impossible, so far as I can see, in some people seeing that which is invisible to others. If the objects are indeed there, and if the inventive power of the human brain is turned upon the problem, it is likely that some sort of psychic spectacles, inconceivable to us at the moment, will be invented, and that we shall all be able to adapt ourselves to the new conditions.

Doyle then describes how in May 1920 he heard through Mr Gow, the editor of *Light* magazine, 'that alleged photographs of fairies had been taken.' The matter was investigated by a Mr Edward L. Gardner, president of a branch of The Theosophical Society, a member of its executive committee and a lecturer in that subject, whom his sister Miss Gardner describes as a theosophist. The photograph was taken by sixteen-year old Elsie Wright in the woods near her home in the village of Cottingley near Bingley in Yorkshire, in company with her cousin Frances Griffiths, aged ten. Elsie had borrowed her father's camera for the purpose.

Knowing of Doyle's interest in such matters, Miss E. Blomfield (a friend of the Gardner family) sent two of the photographs to Doyle who set about trying to determine their authenticity. Doyle now travelled to London to meet Gardner who showed him the 'beautiful enlargements of these two wonderful pictures....'³ Gardner subsequently informed Doyle that he had shown the negatives of the photographs to a Mr Snelling of Harrow: a man of great experience who had worked for over thirty years at a photographic factory. Snelling pronounced that one exposure only had been taken (i.e. nothing had been superimposed in order to effect a deception), and that 'all the figures of the fairies moved during exposure ... ' (which implied that the fairies were living creatures!) Doyle confirmed this by taking the photographic negatives to the Kodak company offices at Kingsway where another expert declared that he could find 'no evidence of superposition, or other tricks.' In other words, the photographs were considered to be genuine.⁴

On 31 July 1920, Gardner wrote to Doyle saying that he had travelled north and interviewed Elsie's father Arthur Wright. Doyle himself now travelled to Yorkshire where he interviewed Mrs Wright, her daughter Elsie and Elsie's cousin Frances (who featured in the first photograph). He was also quick to assert that the photographs were genuine:.'To the objections of photographers that the fairy figures showed quite different shadows to those of the human, our answer is that ectoplasm, as the etheric protoplasm has been named, has a faint luminosity of its own, which would largely modify shadows.⁵'

In September 1920, Gardner was again in communication with Doyle who was currently visiting Melbourne, Australia, sending to him by post, in Doyle's words, 'three more wonderful prints, all taken [by Elsie and Frances] in the fairy glen. Any doubts which had remained in my mind as to honesty were completely overcome ... '⁶ Doyle then goes on to describe how he had received reports from all over the world from people who have allegedly seen fairies, including Texas, USA; the Isle of Man; New Zealand; and Canada.

In his book, Doyle quotes Gardner, 'Since he is both the discoverer of the fairies and a considerable authority on theosophic teaching':

Fairies use bodies of identity that we should describe, in non-technical language, as of a lighter than gaseous nature ... Fairies are not born and do not die as we do, though they have their periods of outer activity and retirement. There is little or no mentality awake [which presumably means that the fairies have no thought processes during their waking hours] – simply a gladsome, irresponsible joyousness of life that is abundantly in evidence in their enchanting abandon. There is no food taken, as we should regard it. Nourishment, usually abundant and ample for sustenance, is absorbed directly by a rhythmical beating or pulse. Resource to the magnetic bath on occasion appears to be their only special restorative.

Doyle concludes the case of the Cottingley fairy photographs by saying that as regards the evidence:

There is enough already available to convince any reasonable man that the matter is not one which can be readily dismissed, but that a case actually exists which up to now has not been shaken in the least degree by any of the criticism directed against it. Far from being resented, such criticism, so long as it is earnest and honest, must be most welcome to those whose only aim is the fearless search for truth.[7]

In 1971, when BBC Televison's Nationwide programme took up the case and spent ten days investigating the circumstances, Elsie Wright – now Mrs Elsie Hill – all but admitted that her fairy story had been a hoax. The BBC interviewer suggested to Elsie that the reason she now felt able to speak freely might be connected with the fact that Edward Gardner had died the previous year. To this, Elsie immediately concurred saying, 'I didn't want to upset Mr Gardner … I don't mind talking now … .' When the interviewer intimated that her father may have colluded with her in the matter, she sprang to his defence:

'I would swear on the Bible father didn't know what was going on,' she said.
Interviewer: 'Could you equally swear on the Bible you didn't play any tricks?'
Elsie (after a pause): 'I took the photographs … I took two of them … no, three … . Frances took two … .' Interviewer: 'Are they trick photographs? Could you swear on the Bible about that?'
Elsie (after a pause): 'I'd rather leave that open if you don't mind … but my father had nothing to do with it I can promise you that … .'
Interviewer: 'Have you had your fun with the world for 50 years? Have you been kidding us for 10 days?'
(Elsie laughs.) Elsie (gently): 'I think we'll close on that if you don't mind.'[8]

By 1981, Frances Griffiths – now Mrs Frances Way, aged seventy-four, had been interviewed by psychic researcher Joe Cooper. She claimed that the first four photographs taken had been faked. 'I could see the hatpins holding up the figures. I've always marvelled that anybody took it seriously,' she said. She maintained, however, that the fifth one was real.[9]

In June 1982, Elsie Hill, who was now aged eighty-one, wrote to the managing director of Sothebys' auctioneers in London offering to sell her account of the story of the fairies of Cottingley, which she described as having been a 'practical joke'. In her letter she referred sympathetically to Doyle, saying:

> He had lost a son recently in the war [First World War], and I think the poor man was trying to comfort himself in these things, so I said to Frances, 'We are a lot younger than Conan Doyle and Mr Gardner, so we will wait till they die of old age and then we will tell.'[10]

It is suggested that the fairies depicted in the photographs were in fact drawings which Elsie had made, possible sources being *Princess Mary's Gift Book* (containing drawings of fairies by Arthur Shepperson), *In the Fairy Ring* by Florence Harrison or *The Fairies* by William Allingham (illustrated by E. Gertrude Thompson). Fairies similar to those depicted in the photographs were also featured in an advertisement for 'Price's Night Lights' (i.e. candles). The other possibility is that the girls had cut the figures out of the books with a sharp pair of scissors, and secured them with hatpins to fronds of foliage growing in Cottingley woods. The photographs having been taken, the cut-outs were then deliberately dropped into the stream to destroy the evidence.[11]

* * *

Doyle's determination to believe that fairy phenomena such as those described above were genuine, may perhaps explain his interest and admiration for several authors who included the subject of fairies in their literary works: in particular J.M. Barrie. This interest of Doyle's is revealed by the Reverend John Lamond, DD, who described a conversation that he had with Doyle in 1925:

> Lamond: The subject of fairies might well interest every Scotsman, for Scotland is pre-eminently the land of the fairies. James Hogg, the

Ettrick Shepherd, wrote the finest fairy poetry in the world. You have doubtless read his *Bonny Kilmeny*?

Doyle: Yes, Hogg was a remarkable man, a kind of second [Robert] Burns in his way. His ballads almost equal those of Sir Walter [Scott].

Lamond: Sir Walter had always a profound interest in the supernormal. In his Introduction to the *Ballad of Tamlane* he goes fully into the subject of fairy lore. The *Ballad of Tamlane* gives a vivid glimpse of those changes of personality that were attributed to the fairies. The capturing of children by the, 'wee fouk [folk]' was widely believed in Scotland. You will remember that [J.M.] Barrie works out the same idea in *Mary Rose*.

Doyle: Barrie knows the secret. He himself is the child of the fairies. Think of the phenomenal success that has attended alike his literary and dramatic efforts. There is no position in literature to which he may not attain. As to Sir Walter, what has struck me in all his writings is the fact that behind alike his poetry and prose there is in almost every volume the recognition of the supernormal.... The same is true of Shakespeare and Goethe. The ghost in Hamlet, the fairies in Midsummer Night's Dream, the dissolving pageants in The Tempest – indeed, throughout the writings of Shakespeare there is the recognition of an inner mysterious world that transcends ordinary observation. I do not need to remind you of Mephistopheles in Faust. The same is true of Dante. All our great creative minds are at one in this respect, confirming the Jewish scriptures that there may be grades of being beyond our recognition, and worlds beyond worlds and within worlds which we can only dimly sense. [12]

In regard to the fairies, Doyle declared that, 'It is not everyone who sees them. It is only a man or woman in ten thousand that has ever had such an experience.'[13] Therefore, when he referred to Barrie knowing 'the secret', this is what he was referring to. In fact, Doyle and Barrie were to become great friends. They played cricket together and Barrie was a guest at Doyle's marriage to Jean Leckie. So did Barrie, the author of the dramatic fantasy story *Peter Pan*, which featured the fairy 'Tinker Bell', also believe in fairies? The answer is, probably not, for as author David Stashower points out, 'Barrie made it perfectly clear that he would not permit any discussion of psychic matters in his presence'.

# Harry Houdini: Further Psychic Experiences

Doyle was a great admirer of the legendary escapologist Harry Houdini whom he and his wife had met in 1920 in Portsmouth, UK when they watched him perform one of his great escapes: this time from within a crate, in which he had been incarcerated wearing a straightjacket. In the chapter entitled 'The Riddle of Houdini', in his book *The Edge of the Unknown*, Doyle quotes from 'the late Mr Hewat Mackenzie, one of the most experienced psychical researchers in the world,' who describes how Houdini escaped from a water-filled tank even though it was covered with an iron lid, fastened with three hasps and staples. These, and other feats of Houdini, said Doyle, show that 'his powers really covered the whole field of what we associate with physical mediumship in its strongest form, and can be covered so far as I can see by no other explanation whatsoever.'[1]

To Doyle's way of thinking, Houdini effected his escapes by 'dematerial-izing' – in other words, turning himself into ectoplasm and simply oozing free of the handcuffs, straightjackets or packing crates which confined him. Said Houdini, '… Arthur thinks that I have great mediumistic powers, and that some of my feats are done with the aid of spirits.' He then tried to disillusion Doyle, telling him frankly and openly that, 'Everything I do is accomplished by material means, humanly possible, no matter how baffling it is to the layman.'[2] However Doyle would have none of it and believed that Houdini was simply being modest.

The two met again during Doyle's lecture tour of America in 1922 when Doyle and his wife Jean were joined at The Ambassador Hotel in Atlantic City by Houdini and his wife Beth for a séance, in which Jean claimed to be in contact with Houdini's mother Cecilia Weiss. Jean wrote down no fewer than fifteen pages of the message, which she alleged she had received from Weiss. Houdini was unmoved. 'I sat serene through it all, hoping, wishing, that I might feel my mother's presence. There wasn't even a semblance of it.'[3]

The writing down of messages from the dead in this fashion is called 'automatic', or 'trance' writing; something which Doyle makes mention of in his book *The New Revelation* (published in 1918), where, referring to a period late in 1915 he writes:

> I have had some very exceptional opportunities of confirming all the views which I had already formed as to the truth of the general facts upon which my views are founded. These opportunities came through the fact that a lady who lived with us, a Mrs L.S., developed the power of automatic writing.

The 'Mrs L.S.' referred to is in fact Doyle's wife Jean's friend Lily Loder-Symonds. In 1926, Doyle wrote:

> It is now five years since the great gift of inspired writing first came to my wife. In her intense honesty and deep modesty, she somewhat retarded it at first by holding back her impulses in the fear lest they should come from her own subconscious self. Gradually, however, the unexpected nature of the messages, and the allusions to be found in them showed both her and me that there were forces at work which were outside herself.[4]

In other words, it appears that Jean learned the technique from Lily and began to practise it from 1921 onwards. Lily, it has to be said, had a vested interest in contacting the dead, having lost three of her brothers in the First World War.

Lily alleged that she had received a message from Malcolm Leckie, Jean's deceased brother. As for Jean Doyle, she also claimed to have received messages from Malcolm Leckie, from Doyle's late sister Annette and from his late brother Innes. Significantly, however, no message was ever reported to have arrived from Doyle's first wife Louise.[5]

* ★ *

In 1920–21, Doyle visited Australia and New Zealand in order to promote his beliefs in spiritualism. He was therefore abroad, when on 30 December

1920, his mother Mary died aged eighty-three. To the end, she had remained sceptical about her son's beliefs; Doyle stating that, 'For my own psychic work she had, I fear, neither sympathy nor understanding ... '[6]

In April 1922, Doyle took Jean (and the three younger children) to the USA, where in New York they attended a séance conducted by William R. Thompson and his wife Eva. Here, Doyle's mother made her presence felt, both spiritually and physically. Dr Leonard J. Hartman, a trustee of the first Spiritualist Church of New York, said that afterwards Doyle had declared, 'The chance to touch my mother's hand and feel the substance there; the chance to see her force, was very precious to me.'[7] Three days later, the Thompsons were arrested by the police and charged with fraud; the so-called spirit, which had resided in a cabinet, proving in fact to be Mrs Thompson herself.

When, in 1922, spirit photographer William Hope was exposed as a fraud, Doyle rushed to his defence; spirit photography being defined by Doyle as 'the remarkable power of producing extra faces, figures, or objects upon photographic plates.'[8] On 10 December 1922, a message arrived from a spirit guide who introduced himself as Pheneas, an Arab who had once been a scribe of the city Ur in Sumeria (in present day Iraq), and had lived some 3,000 years before Christ. Pheneas told Doyle that he (Doyle), 'had been chosen to make spiritualism universally understood.'[9] The spirit guide now became a regular feature at séances held at Windlesham with Doyle, Jean and the children in attendance. It was through Pheneas that Doyle's deceased family and friends were able to describe to him the joys and pleasures of the afterlife. Doyle subsequently chronicled his experiences and published them in 1927 under the title of *Pheneas Speaks*.

Pheneas encouraged Doyle to persevere in his attempts to convert others to spiritualism. 'Go on as you are doing. Their unbelief will fall as a dark garment from them.'[10] It was he who suggested in 1925, that Doyle and his wife purchase another house. On the down side however, Pheneas predicted a 'harvest time' where a great global catastrophe would befall the Earth.

The spring of 1923 found Doyle and his family once more in the USA and also in Canada. In October 1923, the *Strand Magazine* began serialising Doyle's autobiography *Memories and Adventures* (published the following year by John Murray). In 1925, Doyle took the advice of his spirit guide Pheneas and purchased Bignell Wood, near Minstead in Hampshire's New Forest, as a retreat. From now on, he and his wife divided their time between this property and Windlesham. Late that year Doyle opened a psychic bookshop in London's Victoria Street; attended a meeting of the International Spiritualist Congress in Paris of which he was chairman, and had his psychic novel *The Land of Mist* serialised in *The Strand Magazine*. In it, Professor Challenger, who had previously featured in *The Lost World* and *The Poison Belt*, is converted to spiritualism. 1928 found Doyle and his family in South Africa promoting the cause of spiritualism.

Now Doyle devoted the same amount of energy to writing about spiritualism as he had done previously in respect of his historical, romantic, and detective novels. Books on this subject include: *The Wanderings of a Spiritualist* (1921); *The History of Spiritualism* (1926); *Pheneas Speaks: Direct Spirit Communications in the Family Circle* (1927). Doyle's last book *The Edge of the Unknown* (1930), was a collection of previously published essays on spiritualism.

★ ★ ★

Doyle's autobiography leaves the reader in no doubt whatsoever of his personal, first-hand experience of psychic phenomena, in auditory, visual, tactile and olfactory forms:

> In the presence of Miss Besinnet as medium and of several witnesses I have seen my mother and my nephew, young Oscar Hornung, as plainly as ever I saw them in life – so plainly that I could almost have counted the wrinkles of the one and the freckles of the other.
>
> In the darkness the face of my mother shone up, peaceful, happy, slightly inclined to one side, the eyes closed. My wife upon my right and the lady upon my left both saw it as clearly as I did. The lady had not known my mother in life but she said, 'How wonderfully like she is to her son,' which will show how clear was the detail of the features.
>
> On another occasion my son came back to me. Six persons heard his conversation with me, and signed a paper afterwards to that effect. My brother, General Doyle, came back with the same medium, but on another occasion. All fine-drawn theories of the subconscious go to pieces before the plain statement of the intelligence, 'I am a spirit. I am Innes. I am your brother.'
>
> I have clasped materialized hands. I have held long conversations with the direct voice. I have smelt the peculiar ozone-like smell of ectoplasm. I have listened to prophecies which were quickly fulfilled. I

have seen the 'dead' glimmer up upon a photographic plate which no hand but mine had touched. I have received through the hand of my own wife, notebooks full of information which was utterly beyond her ken. I have seen heavy articles swimming in the air, untouched by human hand, and obeying directions given to unseen operators. I have seen spirits walk round the room in fair light and join in the talk of the company. I have known an untrained woman possessed by an artist spirit, and rapidly produce a picture now hanging in my drawing-room which few living painters could have bettered.

I have read books which might have come from great thinkers and scholars, and which were actually written by unlettered men who acted as the medium of the unseen intelligence, so superior to his own. I have recognized the style of a dead writer which no parodist could have copied, and which was written in his own handwriting. I have heard singing beyond earthly power, and whistling done with no pause for the intake of breath. I have seen objects from a distance projected into a room with closed doors and windows.[11]

The next question is, what credibility, if any, do modern scholars attach to the subject of psychic phenomena?

# The Paranormal:
# The Present Position

Consultant statistician Dr Christopher Scott describes, under the heading *Paranormal Phenomena: the Problem of Proof*, the difficulty in evaluating the paranormal from the:

> ... wide range of reported phenomena called 'supernatural'. These ranged from, ghosts to levitation, and included thought-reading, séance-room 'materialization', water-divining, communications with the dead, precognition, hypnosis (arguably), and a long list of others. Did these phenomena really exist, and if they did, why did they seem to stay so stubbornly, outside the scientific world-view?[1]

Psychologist John Beloff writes:

> The group of scientists and scholars who came together in 1882 to found the Society for Psychical Research in London ... were all acutely aware of the materialistic implications of contemporary science and were no less convinced of the futility of trying to counter it with a reaffirmation of the dogmas of revealed religion. They believed, however, that it might still be possible to defend the autonomy of mind, as distinct from brain, if the objective methodology of science were to be deployed in the study of so-called paranormal phenomena.

Despite this, Beloff concurs with Scott's view, stating that 'It is an astounding fact, that a century after the founding of *The Society for Psychical Research*, there is still a total lack of consensus regarding the actuality of any parapsychological phenomenon.'[2]

Of the distinguished members of the *Society for Psychical Research* who were attempting to discover the whereabouts of the spirits of the dead, Scientific Officer Christopher Evans had this to say:

> Their unbinding enthusiasm for their findings led other, more critical and sceptical colleagues to conduct their own experiments. The result was that medium after medium was exposed as fraudulent, the pioneers were shown up to be gullible, incompetent, or both, and this phase of psychical research, which had fleetingly looked as though it might have revolutionary importance, came to an inglorious end.[3]

Evans is also clearly in agreement with the views expressed above:

> While it is true that many feel that parapsychology or psychical research is still a legitimate area of study, most scientists who have studied the topic in any depth are inclined to the view that a hundred years of fairly dedicated research has yielded disappointingly little in an area which should have offered great riches.[4]

Finally, Scott states the present position to be as follows:

> With the single exception of hypnosis not even the existence of one of the phenomena originally classed as supernatural, or later as paranormal, has achieved general acceptance among the scientific community; not one demonstrable, or repeatable, paranormal fact has been discovered; not one characteristic or law has been found which turns up in all those experiments that claim a positive result.[5]

★   ★   ★

Under the heading *Paranormal Phenomena and the Unconscious*, C.W. Wilson, an author from Cornwall, UK, describes the attempts by the Toronto Society for Psychical Research to *create* a ghost in 1972:, 'The experiment seemed to confirm a theory, long held by many parapsychologists: that psychical phenomena originate in the subconscious minds of human beings.'[6] In this brief statement, Wilson has come to the very heart of the matter by proposing that, whereas in the past scholars have devoted much time and energy in efforts (largely, if not wholly fruitless) to *explain* paranormal phenomena, insufficient attention has been given to the possibility that psychic visions, voices, aromas, sensations and so forth may be internal phenomena *created within the human brain itself.*

★   ★   ★

Is it possible to reconcile Doyle's categorical statements about personally witnessing paranormal phenomena and believing in fairies, with the intense scepticism that exists in modern scientific circles about the validity of spiritualism? The answer is no, and the only possible conclusion is that Doyle was suffering from hallucinations (perceptions that occur when there is no external stimulus), and delusions (fixed, irrational ideas not shared by others and not responding to reasoned argument).

Can it therefore be concluded that all mediums and attenders of séances who say they have experienced paranormal phenomena can be said to be suffering from the same condition as Doyle? Probably not, given the fact that he himself recognised many mediums are charlatans who indulge their trade for reasons such as self aggrandisement or pecuniary gain. Also, the skilled medium knows full well that his or her task is simply to convince a receptive audience of something which it is longing to believe anyway – i.e. that their deceased loved ones are happy and still able to communicate with them, despite the apparent obstacle created by death. In other words, the medium is half-way towards his objective before he even begins his work.

Is it possible that as far as his hallucinations were concerned, Doyle was duped by those mediums with whom he came into contact, including his second wife Jean? Author Georgina Doyle (daughter of Doyle's brother Innes) certainly believes that, 'imagination and wishful thinking augmented any real power she may have had,' and that it is impossible to know how much is genuine and how much is Jean's imagination. It appears, in some respects, as if Jean was using the séances to get all she wanted such as trips abroad with Arthur and the children, and Bignell Wood, the cottage in the New Forest.[7] So given the possibility that Jean and other mediums with whom Doyle came into contact acted as the vehicle by which he communicated with the world of the paranormal is it also possible that he suffered from hallucinations?

Hallucinations are categorised by psychiatrists into various subtypes:[8]

## AUDITORY HALLUCINATIONS

'May be experienced as noises, music, or voices. Voices may be heard clearly or indistinctly; they may seem to speak words, phrases, or sentences. Sometimes the voices seem to speak the patient's thoughts as he is thinking them, or to repeat them immediately after he has thought them'. (This is perhaps the best available description of what a [genuine] medium experiences during a séance – i.e. hearing a voice which is simply a reflection of his own thoughts.)

*Doyle: 'I have heard singing beyond earthly power.' 'I am a spirit. I am Innes. I am your brother.'*

## VISUAL HALLUCINATIONS

*Doyle: 'I have seen my mother and my nephew … as plainly as ever I saw them in life.'*

## OLFACTORY AND GUSTATORY HALLUCINATIONS

*Doyle: 'I have smelt the peculiar ozone-like smell of ectoplasm.'*

## TACTILE HALLUCINATIONS

*Doyle: 'I have clasped materialized hands.'*

Delusions are categorised in much the same way, some of the subtypes described being particularly applicable to Doyle.[9]

## DELUSIONS OF REFERENCE

False beliefs, 'that objects, events, or people, unconnected with the patient, have a personal significance for him.'

THE SIGN OF FOUR

Who murdered Sholto? The last and highest court of appeal in detection - Sherlock Holmes - was roused to solve that problem - and solved it.

Arthur Conan Doyle

1 *The Sign of Four*, 1924 edition.

HOUND of the BASKERVILLES"
By Sir A. Conan Doyle.

POPULAR NOVELS ILLUSTRATED

BASKERVILLES

2 *The Hound of the Baskervilles*. Edwardian promotional postcard.

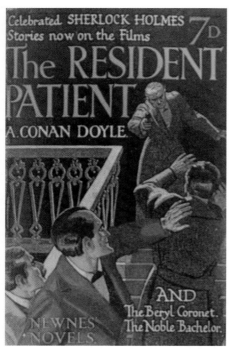

3 *The Resident Patient*, 1921 edition.

4 *The Man with the Twisted Lip*, 1921 edition.

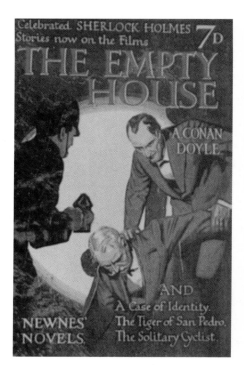

5 *The Empty House*, 1921 edition.

6 *The Adventures of Sherlock Holmes*: Player's Cigarettes.

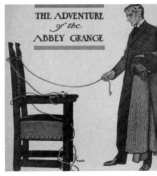

*Left:* 7 Sherlock Holmes Puzzle: Gallaher's Cigarettes.

*Above:* 8 *The Adventure of the Abbey Grange*: Cover for Collier's, 31 December 1904.

9 Universal Studios film poster, 1942–1946.

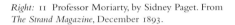
*Above:* 10 *The Adventure of the Missing Three-Quarter*. Cover for Collier's, 26 November 1904.

*Right:* 11 Professor Moriarty, by Sidney Paget. From *The Strand Magazine*, December 1893.

12 Blairerno House (before it was destroyed by fire in 1993).

IS THIS A GIRL OR A CAT?
OR BOTH?

*Above:* 13 View of Carmont Hill from Blairerno House.

*Left:* 14 'Is this a girl or a cat? Or both? I have known such a creature', by Charles Doyle, from his *Diary*.

*Above:* 15 'Sunnyside', by Charles Doyle, from his *Diary*.

*Left:* 16 Floral display, Sunnyside, by Charles Doyle, from his *Diary*.

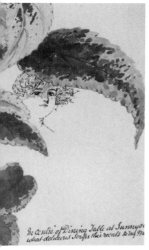

In centre of Dining Table at Sunnyside
what delicious Soufes this recals to us Ma

17 Crichton Royal Hospital
in 1847, from an original oil
painting by Joseph Watson of
Dumfries.

18 'Enter, an Elf in search of a Fairy', by Richard Doyle, from his book, *In Fairy Land*.

19 'He finds her, and this is the consequence', by Richard Doyle, from his book, *In Fairy Land*.

*For Doyle, this could apply to his view of mediums, fairies, and in particular, of the spirit guide, Pheneas.*

## DELUSIONS OF CONTROL

Where a subject, 'believes that his actions, impulses, or thoughts are controlled by an outside agency.'[10]

*For Doyle, perhaps the word 'control' is too strong, but he was certainly influenced by voices from the spirit world.*

## GRANDIOSE DELUSIONS

'Are beliefs of exaggerated self-importance. The patient may think him or herself wealthy, endowed with unusual abilities, or [to be] a special person.' He or she, '… may believe that they are religious prophets destined to advise statesmen about great issues.'[11]

*This applies to Doyle, in the sense that he produced numerous books on spiritualism and travelled the world giving lecture tours to convince everyone that he was right. 'God had placed me in a very special position for conveying it [i.e. the spiritualistic knowledge of 'the continuation of life'] to that world which needed it so badly,'[12] he said.*

\* \* \*

So yes, Doyle may well have been duped by various mediums but the above evidence, together with his own vivid descriptions of his experiences, points to the fact that he was suffering from a significant psychiatric disorder which apparently began to afflict him only in later life. So what type of disorder might this have been?

A Possible Diagnosis: hallucinations occur in diverse disorders: notably schizophrenia, organic (physical) disorders, dissociative states (disruption of the usually integrated functions of consciousness, memory, identity or perception)[13] and severe mood disorder.[14] Of these, the first three can probably be ruled out in Doyle's case (the chronic schizophrenic being characterised typically by, 'underactivity, lack of drive, social withdrawal and emotional apathy, and … thought disorder.')[15]

Delusions indicate serious mental illness such as schizophrenia or mania.

Delusions are classified as primary which appear, 'suddenly and with full conviction but without any mental events leading up to it [i.e. them]';[16] or secondary which are, 'apparently derived from a preceding morbid [unwholesome] experience.' Primary delusions, 'are given considerable weight in the diagnosis of schizophrenia ... .'[17] Doyle's delusions however, were of the secondary variety, suggesting the diagnosis of mania rather than schizophrenia.

The following would appear to be highly relevant:

> The essence of the modern concept of delusional disorder is that of a hitherto stable delusional system developing insidiously in a person in middle or late life. The delusional system is encapsulated, and there is no impairment of other mental functions. The patient can often go on working, and his social life may be maintained fairly well. Delusional disorder is regarded as being an uncommon illness, although there are relatively few data.[18]

This description would appear to fit Doyle like the proverbial glove, in that yes, he did continue to write his books, pursue his correspondence, enjoy a happy family life, walks and recreation, despite his mental condition. So was mania the cause of Doyle's delusional and hallucinatory disorder?

*Mania* is characterised by 'elevation of mood, increased activity and self-important ideas.'[19] Certainly, it is difficult to imagine how anyone could have fitted more into a single lifespan than Doyle and some might argue that this was a reflection of a manic personality (or at least hypomanic – i.e. one who displays mania in a mild form). Yet others might say that Doyle was simply a highly energetic and industrious person. There is, of course, ample evidence of his self-important ideas.

Another feature of the more severe manic states is that insight is invariably impaired. 'Patients ... seldom think of themselves as ill or in need of treatment.'[120]That Doyle had no insight into his own condition is borne out by a statement he made about spiritualism:

> When I talk on this subject, I'm not talking about what I believe, I'm not talking about what I think, I'm talking about what I know. There's an enormous difference between believing a thing and knowing a thing. I'm talking about things that I've handled, that I've seen, that I've heard

with my own ears, and always mind you, in the presence of witnesses.[21] (Mania may co-exist with depression, in which case it is called bipolar disorder. However, there is little evidence to show that Doyle was a depressive).

To summarise, an appropriate description of Doyle would appear to be a person displaying an encapsulated delusional disorder, probably as a consequence of inherent mania which manifested itself in later life as the condition typically does.

# Charles Doyle: Like Father, Like Son?

In attempting to discover the reason for the strange behaviour of Doyle in his later life, it seems logical first to examine the life of his father Charles, who was himself afflicted by mental illness which until now was believed to have been self-induced by his excessive and prolonged consumption of alcohol.

As already stated, it was in the year 1879 that Charles was admitted to Blairerno House, the home for intemperates [i.e. drunkards] near Drumlithie in north-east Scotland.[1] (Several authors have mistakenly referred to Fordoun House as being the home for intemperates. This house does exist but it has always been in private hands and it was never an institution).

Blairerno House, situated on a hillside above a stream called Carron Water, was built in 1691. Roughly cruciform in layout, the house was added to until there were seventeen rooms in all. Included on the ground floor was a 'Rayburn room' (named after the type of stove used to heat it), where the bells by which the boarders could summon the staff were situated, a large sitting room with bay window and a priest's hole (a secret room for the priest in times of persecution or repression). Above, several rooms with dormer windows had been built into the roof space. Views from the house were restricted on account of outbuildings which included three bothys (furnished cottages), in one of which the male farm servants were housed. However, from the upper floors could be seen the rounded shape of the 1,300ft high Carmont Hill away to the east.[2] Many more hills lay to the north beyond Fetteresso Forest and also to the west.

In the 1860s and 1870s, the proprietor of the Lawgavan Estate of which Blairerno was a part, was James Cumine Burnett of Monboddo, who leased the property and farm to tenants. According to the valuation rolls, in 1878/9, the tenant was James Forbes and the occupier was David Forbes.[3] The 1871 census indicates that David Forbes (who was James's brother), was a cattle breeder and that he lived at Blairerno House with his wife, their two daughters and his two sisters.

The property appears to have begun operating as a home for intemperates from about the year 1881, when according to the census, there were two (male) boarders in residence: Stuart Milne, a thirty-two year old former bank clerk, and John MacFarline, a twenty-five year old former army officer. In 1882, the following advertisement appeared in the *Medical Directory*:

> INTEMPERANCE – Home for Gentlemen in Country House in the North of Scotland. Of very old standing. Home Comforts. Good Shooting [David Forbes having acquired the shooting rights from the local Lawgaven Estate], Trout-Fishing and Cricket. HIGHEST REFERENCES. Apply MR D FORBES, BLAIRERNO HOUSE, DRUMLITHIE, FORDOUN, KINCARDINESHIRE.[4]

(The *Medical Directory* contained more information about individual members of the medical profession than was to be found in the *Medical Register*, it being a kind of 'Who's Who' of the medical profession. It also carried advertisements for medical textbooks and equipment, furniture designed for the disabled ('invalids'), and so forth. Advertisements such as the one above for Homes for Intemperates invariably ran into several pages, indicating just how common a problem alcoholism was in those days.)

Blairerno House was clearly a high-class establishment. However, the concept of the inebriates roaming around with loaded guns in their possession is a somewhat alarming one!

\* \* \*

Blairerno House was a private institution and no patient records exist from that time. However, according to the 1881 Census it was occupied by David Forbes, aged forty-seven, a farmer of 221 acres (who had evidently taken over the farm from his brother James) employing three men and three boys; his wife Marianne also aged forty-seven; their daughter Elizabeth, aged sixteen; David's two unmarried sisters, Mary Anne, aged fifty-five, and Elizabeth, aged fifty-three. Also listed at Blairerno House are eighteen male boarders, who were mainly professional people; the youngest aged twenty-five and an MA of Edinburgh University, and the oldest aged sixty-seven and a retired bank clerk. The list also includes two officers in the armed forces (one retired); a landed proprietor; a medical student (William L.S. Wright, from England, who evidently never qualified as a doctor as his name does not appear subsequently in the Medical Register); a teacher of music; a tobacco manufacturer; a retired ship owner; a West India (Company) merchant; two annuitants (those in receipt of an annuity); and, of course, Charles Doyle, aged forty-nine and described as, 'Architect and Artist'. Ten of the boarders were born in Scotland, six in England, one in Spain and one in Sydney, Australia.

Although David Forbes was the proprietor of the home it was probably his two sisters Mary and Elizabeth who ran it, assisted by a household staff consisting of cook, kitchen maid, laundry maid, housemaid and table maid: all of whom are listed on the census. It is difficult to see how the boarders and the Forbes family could all have been accommodated in Blairerno House and it is possible that some of the former were housed in two of the adjacent bothys. Also, David Forbes rented a house and a croft in the nearby village of Drumlithie, so perhaps he lived here for some of the time.[5]

In 1882, Dr Arthur Burt, aged thirty-seven, a graduate of Edinburgh University and a bachelor, arrived at Blairerno House from Edinburgh's Balgreen Asylum as a boarder. Having a doctor on the premises, albeit an inebriate, was doubtless an advantage. For example, when Henry Carr (a fellow boarder), drowned in the bath following an epileptic fit, Burt was able to sign the death certificate. (Three years later, Burt would marry proprietor David Forbes' younger sister Elizabeth. Sadly, the marriage was short lived for in March 1888, Burt's past caught up with him and he died of liver and stomach cancer, a well known complication of alcoholism.) Soon, Charles Doyle himself would be afflicted by epilepsy – which is another known complication of alcoholism. This was of such severity that it would have catastrophic consequences for him.

*     *     *

So what had necessitated Charles's admission to Blairerno House, where he was to stay for a period of six years (and where alcohol was presumably totally denied to him)?

In his autobiography Doyle suggests that even from an early age his father Charles had been somewhat over-fond of drink. Describing the time in about 1850 when Charles, then aged eighteen, was sent from London to Edinburgh (where he obtained lodgings with Kathleen Foley, mother of Mary, whom he would one day marry), Doyle said, 'The Scottish society … into which he [Charles] had been precipitated at a dangerously early age … [was] rough, hard-drinking, and kindly.'[6]

Also in his autobiography, Doyle describes how his mother Mary bore the 'long, sordid strain' of life in Edinburgh, where, 'we lived in the hardy and bracing atmosphere of poverty ….' 'My father, I fear, was of little help to her, for his thoughts were always in the clouds and he had no appreciation of the realities of life.'[7]

A letter dated 3 December 1892, from Mary Doyle at Masongill Cottage, Masongill, North Yorkshire to Dr James Rutherford, Physician Superintendent at Crichton Royal Hospital, demonstrates that in his autobiography Doyle had merely alluded to what, in fact, was an extremely serious situation (her punctuation and spelling):

My poor husband's condition was brought on by drink. He has had delirium tremens [convulsions, tremors and hallucinations brought on by alcohol] several times. Just thirty years ago – Decr. 62 [December 1862, when Charles was aged 30] – he had such a bad attack that for nearly a year he had to be on half pay and for months he cd [could] only crawl and was perfectly idiotic, could not tell his own name. Since then he has been from one fit of dipsomania to another. Using the most awful expedients, many times putting himself within the reach of the law – to get drink – Every article of value he or I possessed [he] carried off secretly, debts to large amount contracted to our trades people, bills given etc. – all for goods which never entered our doors, but were at once converted into money. There is a public house in Edinburgh where I am told they have a most valuable collection of his sketches, given for drink. He would sell for a few pence a sketch worth several guineas. He would strip himself of all his underclothing, take the very bed linen, climb down the water spout at risk of his life, break open the children's money boxes. He even drank furniture varnish. All our friends said the only way to save his life was to out him where he could get no drink. He only kept his position in the office because being <u>very talented</u> he could do what was wanted better than the others and also that his amiable disposition endeared him to our kind friends, Mr. Matheson and Mr. Andrew Kerr, his superiors. To know him was to love him.[8]

Did Charles go to Blairerno House voluntarily? The answer is probably yes, the law at that time being as follows: 'In the Act of 1879 (42 & 42 Vict. Cap. 19), it was affirmed that the habitual drunkard had power by his own act to secure his detention in a licensed institution for a period not exceeding one year, for the purpose of reformation and cure.'[9] In other words, there was at that time no mechanism in place whereby a habitual drunkard could be forcibly detained in a licensed institution (provided that the drunkard in question had committed no criminal offence), let alone an unlicensed one, which Blairerno House evidently was.

How did Charles and the other residents occupy themselves at Blairerno House? Because of their social status it is unlikely that they would have been expected to work, say on the farm. It is more likely that in addition to participating in the recreational activities on offer in David Forbes' advertisement, they would have taken walks; gone on occasional outings; say on the train from nearby New Mill to Stonehaven on the coast or Drumlithie; read books and newspapers; played billiards and cards; and been entertained on the pianoforte. As for Charles himself, it appears that he continued to indulge his talent for artistry, in that several books containing his illustrations were published during this time. They included three children's books: *The Two Bears* (1880), *How the Three Little Pigs Went to Market, and the Old One Stayed at Home* (1880), and *Three Blind Mice* (1883). Also published was the amusingly named *European Slavery* (or *Scenes from Married Life*, 1881).

Sadly, rather than improve at Blairerno House, Charles's condition actually appears to have worsened, as his wife Mary's letter to Dr Rutherford indicates:

I had him at Drumlithie [New Mill] for some years but he broke away always and got drink, then he at last became so violent that two doctors had him certified and put in Montrose Asylum before I knew anything about it. Since then he has been absolutely kept from drink. If he were free again I believe he would kill himself in a few weeks.

I know from his manner you would suppose that he never could behave as I have described (whereas I have only given a few instances) but it was a real madness no doubt. My friend the late Dr. John Brown

... and many others who knew him most intimately said his case was hopeless, the brain being so much affected. One very bad sign was his wonderful mendacity. It seemed as if he cd [could] never speak the truth and yet he was so good, virtuous and pleasant through it all.[10]

As a qualified medical practitioner and also the son of an alcoholic father, Doyle would have been aware more than most of the potentially damaging effects that excessive alcohol intake can have, not only on the person himself, but also on that person's household. It is therefore hardly surprising that the subject of alcoholism and drunkenness should have found its way into his fictional writings. In fact, as will now be seen, these writings appear to reveal more in-depth information about the Doyle family than that which is contained in Doyle's autobiography.

# Charles Revealed through his Son's Writings?

In *The Japanned Box,* it is clear that when the character Richards is discussing the theme of drunkenness, this is in reality Doyle speaking from the heart about something of which he has first-hand knowledge. Richards is land steward to Sir John Bollamore, a widower of Thorpe Place, where a teacher (who narrates the story in the first person), has arrived to tutor Sir John's two young sons. From Richards, the teacher learns of a time when Sir John used to be a drunkard, the land steward going on to give a vivid description of how alcohol may adversely affect a person:

> There is a world of difference, you know, between a man who drinks and a drunkard. They all drink, but they taboo a drunkard. He had become a slave to it —hopeless and helpless. Then she [Sir John's wife] stepped in, saw the possibilities of a fine man in the wreck, took her chance in marrying him, though she might have had the pick of a dozen, and, by devoting her life to it, brought him back to manhood and decency. You have observed that no liquor is ever kept in the house. There never has been any since her foot crossed its threshold. A drop of it would be like blood to a tiger even now.

The teacher describes Sir John as, '... a man who was fighting a ceaseless battle, holding at arm's length, from morning till night, a horrible adversary, who was forever trying to close with him – an adversary which would destroy him body and soul could it but fix its claws once more upon him.' Initially, the teacher believes that he has established a degree of rapport with Sir John, 'In some subtle way he [Sir John] divined the sympathy which I had for him, and he showed in his own silent fashion that he appreciated it. He even invited me once to share his afternoon walk …'

Alas, this happy state of affairs is not to last, for soon comes an incident which leads to the teacher experiencing a 'revulsion of feeling', when he hears the sound of Sir John chastising 'the aged charwoman' of the household:

> It was the snarl of a furious wild beast. Then I heard his voice thrilling with anger. 'You would dare!' he cried. 'You would dare to disobey my directions!' An instant later the charwoman passed me, flying down the passage, white faced and tremulous, while the terrible voice thundered behind her.

Finally, Sir John confides to the teacher how, having become surrounded by false friends, he took to drink:

> My purse suffered, my character suffered, my constitution suffered, stimulants became a necessity to me, I was a creature from whom my memory recoils. And it was at that time, the time of my blackest degradation, that God sent into ray life the gentlest, sweetest spirit that ever descended as a ministering angel from above. She loved me, broken as I was, loved me, and spent her life in making a man once more of that which had degraded itself to the level of the beasts.

(It is highly significant that the word 'stimulants' has been used in this passage, as will be seen shortly.)

In the above account, one cannot fail to notice similarities in the relationship between Sir John and his wife, and between Doyle's father Charles and his mother Mary. Sir John was Charles Doyle: a kind of split personality who was extremely dangerous to others when in the mood, whereas his wife Lady Bollamore, was Mary Doyle, Charles's loving and devoted wife, who found herself trapped in an impossible marriage. The account also implies that Mary was aware of Charles's drink problems *even before* she married him.

★ ★ ★

In Doyle's story *The Beetle Hunter*, the newly qualified doctor Hamilton, who is in lodgings in London, is asked to assist Lord Linchmere in a matter of some delicacy. Linchmere explains that he too is a medical man who devoted some years to medical study before inheriting a peerage. When Linchmere introduces Hamilton to his sister Lady Rossiter, wife of Sir Thomas, an entomologist and the greatest authority upon the subject of beetles in the world, Hamilton makes the following observations:

> Some great grief seemed to have cast its shadow over her features. As Lord Linchmere presented me she turned her face full upon me, and I was shocked to observe a half-healed scar extending for two inches over her right eyebrow. It was partly concealed by plaster, but none the less I could see that it had been a serious wound and not long inflicted.

Linchmere introduces Hamilton to Sir Thomas and the two of them spend the night at the latter's home Delamere Court, keeping watch because Linchmere suspects that Sir Thomas may attack him. Sure enough, in the small hours of the morning Sir Thomas makes a frenzied attack on Linchmere with a heavy hammer. After Hamilton and Linchmere over-power him, the former states that their prisoner now, '… lay foaming and glaring upon the ground. One glance at his face was enough to prove that he was a dangerous maniac, while the short, heavy hammer which lay beside the bed showed how murderous had been his intentions.' Linchmere then takes Hamilton into his confidence:

> My poor brother-in-law is one of the best fellows upon earth, a loving husband and an estimable father, but he comes from a stock which is deeply tainted with insanity. He has more than once had homicidal outbreaks, which are the more painful because his inclination is always to attack the very person to whom he is most attached. His son was sent away to school to avoid this danger, and then came an attempt upon my sister, his wife, from which she escaped with injuries that you may have observed when you met her in London. You understand that he knows nothing of the matter when he is in his sound senses, and would ridicule the suggestion that he could under any circumstances injure those whom he loves so dearly. It is often, as you know, a charac-teristic of such maladies that it is absolutely impossible to convince the man who suffers from them of their existence.

Before each attack, says Linchmere, there are warning signs, in that Sir Thomas:

> ... always shows certain premonitory symptoms, which are providential danger signals, warning us to be upon our guard. The chief of these is that nervous contortion of the forehead which you must have observed. This is a phenomenon which always appears from three to four days before his attacks of frenzy. The moment it showed itself his wife came into town on some pretext, and took refuge in my house in Brooke Street.

In consequence, Linchmere can see 'no other way in which I could remove this terrible danger from my sister's life,' but to have his brother-in-law certified. He therefore asks Hamilton, as a fellow doctor, to sign the 'lunacy papers'.

The true meaning of this purportedly fictional story is obvious. Hamilton, the young doctor, is Doyle; Lord Linchmere, formerly a doctor but now a peer of the realm, is Dr Bryan Charles Waller, who came to lodge with Doyle's mother Mary and family after her husband Charles was committed to a mental institution; Lady Rossiter is Doyle's mother Mary; Sir Thomas is, of course, Doyle's father Charles.

The inevitable conclusion from this thinly veiled allusion by Doyle to his own young life is that Charles had homicidal outbursts in which he threatened his son and his wife Mary; on one occasion attacking her and causing actual bodily harm, for which reason Doyle was sent away to school to escape the danger. *Most significant of all* is the assertion that Sir Thomas – i.e. Charles – came from 'stock' that was 'deeply tainted with insanity,' because this implies that Charles's condition had a hereditary basis.

★ ★ ★

Perhaps the most revealing of all Doyle's allusions to his father are to be found in *The Surgeon of Gaster Fell*, which was published in *Chambers' Journal* in 1890. It is the story of a surgeon J. Cameron and his sister Eva, who have taken their father Cameron senior, to a remote cottage on Gaster Fell in Yorkshire for his own safety and that of others. The drama is recounted by James Upperton who has built himself a cottage on the Fell where he intends to perform 'mystic studies'.

When Upperton meets Eva, he notices that, 'Her face ... wore a weary expression, and her young beauty seemed to be clouded over by the shadow of inward trouble. ... I was conscious of a sudden pang of sympathy and grief as I looked upon the spasm of despair which seemed to convulse this strange and beautiful woman.' Upperton describes Cameron senior as an, 'attenuated creature ... a man of sixty, wrinkled, bent, and feeble, with sparse, grizzled hair, and long, colourless face [with a] cringing, sidelong gait ... ,' whom he sees '... walking rapidly along the hillside, beating the furze bushes with a cudgel and bellowing like a madman. Indeed, at the sight of him, the doubts as to his sanity which had risen in my mind were strengthened and confirmed.' When Cameron senior is restrained and confined to the cottage, Upperton hears him:

> ... pouring forth a stream of words, and moaning from time to time like a man in pain. These words resolved themselves, as I approached, into prayers— shrill, voluble prayers, pattered forth with the intense earnestness of one who sees impending and imminent danger. There was to me something inexpressibly awesome in this gush of solemn entreaty from the lonely sufferer, meant for no human ear, and jarring upon the silence of the night.

When Cameron senior breaks free and approaches Upperton's own cottage, the latter is truly terrified:

> I became aware of a dark, shadowy figure upon my threshold, and of a pale face that looked in at me. The features were human, but the eyes were not. They seemed to burn through the darkness with a greenish brilliancy of their own; and in their baleful, shifty glare I was conscious of the very spirit of murder.

Finally, in a letter to Upperton dated 4 September 1885 and headed 'Kirkby Lunatic Asylum', Cameron junior reveals all:

> My poor father was a hard-working general practitioner in Birmingham, where his name is still remembered and respected. About ten years ago he began to show signs of mental aberration, which we were inclined to put down to overwork and the effects of a sunstroke.
>
> It would weary you were I to describe, the terrible experiences which his family have undergone ... . He has an intense dread of madhouses; and in his sane intervals would beg and pray so piteously not to

be condemned to one, that I could never find the heart to resist him. At last, however, his attacks became so acute and dangerous that I determined, for the sake of those about me, to remove him from the town to the loneliest neighbourhood that I could find ... .YH, poor fellow, was as submissive as a child when in his right mind, and a better, kinder companion no man could wish for ... .[1]

Feeling my own incompetence to pronounce upon a case of such importance, I at once sought the highest advice in Birmingham and London. Among others we consulted the eminent alienist [specialist in mental diseases], Mr. Fraser Brown ...

Brown tells Cameron junior, that in his opinion, his father's condition would continue to be, 'intermittent in its nature, but dangerous during the paroxysms' and that each paroxysm, '... may take a homicidal, or it may take a religious turn, or it may prove to be a mixture of both. You will incur a great responsibility if you leave him without supervision.'

Cameron junior was now in a dilemma:. 'You will understand the terrible task which has fallen upon my poor sister and me in endeavouring to save my father from the asylum which in his sane moments filled him with horror.' Finally however, despite all the efforts of the family, Cameron senior is admitted to the 'Kirkby Lunatic Asylum'. 'Suffice it that, by the blessing of God, we have succeeded in keeping his poor crazed fingers clear of blood,' says Cameron junior.[2]

Once again, the similarities between Cameron senior and Doyle's own father Charles are noticeable. The two are alike in age, physical characteristics and situation. As for Cameron junior, like Doyle he is a medical man with a desperate concern for his father who is mentally ill. The story also leaves no doubt that in his moments of madness the father, and by implication Doyle's father Charles, *is dangerous and even capable of murder.*

There are further parallels in that *The Surgeon of Gaster Fell* is set in the year 1885 and features the escape from confinement of a potentially dangerous person who in those days would be described as a lunatic. Equally, this was the year when Doyle's own father Charles made a violent bid to break out from his own place of confinement, namely Blairerno House.

It is significant, that twenty-five years later, when *The Surgeon of Gaster Fell* was published in book form (by which time his own father Charles had died), Doyle had deleted some of the more intimate of the above passages, presumably because they revealed too much about his family's private life. What the original version of the story *did not* reveal, was whether Charles Doyle, like Cameron senior in the story, had spent time in a lonely moorland cottage. Was this possible, and if so, when was this and where was the cottage?

The setting is a moor near the village of 'Kirkby-Malhouse'. 'Kirkby' was a name which Charles's wife Mary was familiar with, because when she left Edinburgh in 1883 to reside in a cottage on the family estate of her former lodger Bryan Waller, her postal address became 'Masongill Cottage, Kirkby Lonsdale' (the real-life hamlet of Masongill being situated in North Yorkshire, and the village of Kirkby Lonsdale, five miles to the north-east across the border in what was then Westmorland and is now Cumbria). Is it possible that some time before Mary made her move, a cottage was found for Charles to reside in by Bryan Waller on his family's Masongill Estate? If so when might this have been?

As already mentioned, Charles left the Scottish Office of Works in June 1876, but according to his son Doyle, it was not until three years later in 1879 that his father retired to a 'convalescent home'. Could it be that at some time in the interval, Charles resided at Masongill (which, like 'Kirkby-Malhouse', is surrounded by moorland), where he was looked after by his son Doyle and his daughter Annette who would then have been in her twenties? (It has to be said though that Doyle, then a medical student, would probably not have had sufficient time to devote to his father who would have needed constant supervision). And was there an asylum at the real life Kirkby Lonsdale? The answer to the latter question is no, but there was a workhouse which also housed patients with mental problems (there being no institution in Westmorland specifically given over to the care of the mentally ill at that time).[3] However, because of his status it is unlikely that Charles would have been admitted to a workhouse but was he admitted as an emergency case? Whatever the truth may be, his son Doyle was clearly familiar with the name 'Kirkby' and added 'Malhouse' presumably because of that word's similarity to 'Madhouse'.

In *The Surgeon of Gaster Fell*, Doyle has left behind a series of tantalising conundrums, which unlike his Sherlock Holmes stories, may never be solved!

★ ★ ★

So can Charles Doyle's behaviour simply be explained by the fact that he drank; that his drinking led him to become psychotic (suffer from a severe psychiatric disorder), and that this made him aggressive and liable to attack members of his family? Was it as simple as that? There are reasons for suspecting that this idea may be altogether too simplistic, and for the following reasons:

Alcohol-related psychosis is defined as:

> ... a secondary psychosis with predominant hallucinations occurring in many alcohol-related conditions, including acute intoxication, withdrawal, after a major decrease in alcohol consumption, and alcohol idiosyncratic intoxication [that which occurs in a person who is hypersensitive to alcohol].

However, the significant factor as far as Charles Doyle is concerned is that the condition, 'spontaneously clears with discontinuation of alcohol use ... '[4] In Charles's case, however, even though alcohol would have been denied to him over the six year period he spent at New Mill, far from improving, his symptoms got worse.

So what else could have caused his symptoms? Again, the clue is to be found in Doyle's story *The Japanned Box*, when Sir John Bollamore (whose life in many ways mirrors that of Charles Doyle, as demonstrated above) declares that having got into bad company, 'stimulants became a necessity to me.' It might appear fanciful to draw such a conclusion about his father from a fictional work by Doyle, were it not for the existence of a real-life document *which appears to confirm the theory*.

★ ★ ★

A document, signed by Charles's wife Mary some years later, contains some surprising information, because in it she states that the 'Supposed Cause' of her husband's insanity was not his heavy and prolonged drinking but his 'Undue use of Stimulants'.[5] It was therefore probably no coincidence that, as already stated, Doyle used the word 'stimulants' in respect of Sir John Bollamore in *The Japanned Box*. So what might these stimulants have been? Again, a possible answer is to be found in Doyle's novels, and in particular those involving Sherlock Holmes.

# Charles Doyle and the Possible Use of Stimulants

Bearing in mind that the period under discussion is the late nineteenth century, then the word 'stimulant' immediately brings to mind the opiate class of drugs: opium being 'a crude preparation containing at least twenty different alkaloids … .'[1] Of these, the best known are morphine, cocaine and codeine.

L.L. Iverson, Director, Merck, Sharp & Dohme Research Laboratories Ltd, Harlow, UK, points out the attractiveness of opiate drugs, whilst at the same time issuing a caveat, 'They replace the present world with one in which the individual experiences no problems, and often intense pleasure. The most powerful euphoriants – opium and cocaine – are medicinally dangerous drugs: largely because their continued use leads, inevitably, to tolerance and addiction … .'[2]

In his story *The Sign of Four*, Doyle describes his hero Sherlock Holmes' propensity for administering to himself on a regular basis, a seven per cent solution of cocaine, as the latter's chronicler Watson describes:

> Sherlock Holmes took his bottle from the corner of the mantel-piece, and his hypodermic syringe from its neat morocco case. With his long, white, nervous fingers he adjusted the delicate needle, and rolled back his left shirt-cuff. For some little time his eyes rested thoughtfully upon the sinewy forearm and wrist, all dotted and scarred with innumerable puncture-marks. Finally, he thrust the sharp point home, pressed down the tiny piston, and sank back into the velvet-lined arm-chair with a long sigh of satisfaction.

However, Watson makes his disapproval of this habit clear. 'Three times a day for many months I had witnessed this performance, but custom had not reconciled my mind to it.' And Holmes is forced to agree, but with reservations:, 'Perhaps you are right, Watson. I suppose that its influence is physically a bad one. I find it, however, so transcendently stimulating and clarifying to the mind that its secondary action is a matter of small moment.' To which Watson replies:

> But consider! Count the cost! Your brain may, as you say, be roused and excited, but it is a pathological and morbid process, which involves increased tissue-change, and may at last leave a permanent weakness. You know, too, what a black reaction comes upon you. Surely the game is hardly worth the candle. Why should you, for a mere passing pleasure, risk the loss of those great powers with which you have been endowed?

In *The Man With the Twisted Lip*, Watson describes the deleterious effects of drugs in even more graphic detail:

> Isa Whitney, brother of the late Elias Whitney, D.D., Principal of the Theological College of St. George's, was much addicted to opium. The habit grew upon him, as I understand, from some foolish freak when he was at college; for having read De Quincey's [Thomas, English critic and essayist] description of his dreams and sensations, he had drenched his tobacco with laudanum in an attempt to produce the same effects. He found, as so many more have done, that the practice is easier to attain than to get rid of, and for many years he continued to be a slave to the drug, an object of mingled horror and pity to his friends and relatives. I can see him now, with yellow, pasty face, drooping lids, and pin-point pupils, all huddled in a chair, the wreck and ruin of a noble man.

In *A Scandal in Bohemia*, Watson is walking down Baker Street when he notices Holmes':

> ...tall, spare figure pass twice in a dark silhouette against the blind. He was pacing the room swiftly, eagerly, with his head sunk upon his chest and his hands clasped behind him. To me, who knew his every mood

and habit, his attitude and manner told their own story. He was at work again. He had risen out of his drug-created dreams and was hot upon the scent of some new problem.

From Doyle's knowledge of pharmacology gained in his study of medicine, and from the conclusions about the dangers of opiate drugs as articulated vicariously by him via the voice of Dr Watson, it seems highly unlikely that Doyle himself participated in drug taking (although his naturally enquiring mind may have led him to try them on the odd occasion for experimental purposes). If, indeed, Doyle's father Charles did take drugs prior to his admission to Blairerno House, then was Doyle aware of this fact and is this why the subject is mentioned with such frequency in his Sherlock Holmes stories?

Assuming, for a moment that Charles Doyle was addicted to opiates – say cocaine (as well as to alcohol) – prior to his admission to Blairerno House, then what would the likely affect on him have been?

The psychological effects of cocaine include excitement, increased energy and euphoria. This can be associated with grandiose thinking, impaired judgment and sexual disinhibition. Higher doses can result in visual and auditory hallucinations. Paranoid ideation (the power of the mind for forming ideas) may lead to aggressive behaviour. More prolonged use of high doses of cocaine can result in a paranoid psychosis with violent behaviour. This state is usually short-lived but may be more enduring in those with a pre-existing vulnerability to psychotic disorder.

If the preceding cocaine use (by the patient) has been relatively mild, such symptoms resolve within about twenty-four hours. After more prolonged use, the symptoms are more severe and extended, and are associated with intense craving, depression, and occasionally severe suicidal ideation.[3]

A survey of fifty-five cocaine-dependent individuals admitted to the Medical University of South Carolina, USA's Department of Psychiatry, reveals that fifty-three per cent had experienced *transient* cocaine induced psychosis.[4] Therefore, once Charles had been admitted to Blairerno House, one would have expected the acute symptoms described above to disappear (even if the chronic symptoms such as craving, depression, and suicidal thoughts did not). However, the reverse is true. Charles's mental problems *did not disappear*, instead they continued. So if neither alcohol nor opiates were the cause of Charles Doyle's chronic mental health problems, then what was?

\*   \*   \*

In her letter of 3 December 1892 to Dr J. Rutherford, Charles's wife Mary describes her husband's condition as, 'a real madness no doubt.'[5] So, if Charles was suffering from a madness that was intrinsic rather than alcohol or drug induced, then the question is why?

A clue is to be found in Doyle's story *The Beetle Hunter* (mentioned above), where Lord Linchmere says of Sir Thomas Rossiter who has 'more than once had homicidal outbreaks' (one of which involved an attack on his own wife), that he came 'from a stock which is deeply tainted with insanity.' When Doyle wrote about Sir Thomas, was it really his own father whom he had in mind? Did he believe that not only his father Charles but also some of the other members of his family stretching back in time were insane and that this insanity had a hereditary basis?

# The Montrose Royal Asylum

C harles Doyle's medical records give further details of the circumstances leading up to his sudden transfer on 26 May 1885, from Blairerno House to the Montrose Royal Asylum and of his subsequent progress there.

## BLAIRERNO HOUSE, 1879–1885

Referring to Blairerno House which he described not as a home for intemperates but as 'a home for inebriates', Dr Herbert Grealbalch, Assistant Medical Officer at the 'Sunnyside' wing of the Montrose Royal Asylum, declared that during his time spent there, Charles had 'become excited and unmanageable.'[1] It therefore became necessary for Charles to be officially certified as insane under the terms of The Lunacy Acts of 1857 and 1862, for:, 'The regulation of the care and treatment of lunatics, and for the provision, maintenance, and regulation of lunatic asylums in Scotland.'[2] (It is interesting to note that although Charles was officially declared insane in May 1885, his wife Mary [in a document which she signed on 20 January 1892, on the occasion of Charles's being transferred from Montrose Royal Asylum to Edinburgh Royal Asylum], gave his 'length of time insane' as being, 'Since March 1881'.[3] He was then aged forty-nine, and had been a boarder at Blairerno House for two years).

The procedure for having Charles certified as a lunatic was as follows: firstly, a 'petition' to the sheriff was made, 'by the wife or husband or parent, or other relative of the person named … .' In Charles's case, the petition was submitted to William Lowson, Sheriff Substitute of the County of Forfar.

However, the petitioner was not Charles's wife Mary, who was apparently unavailable at the time, or any other member of the family, but David Forbes, proprietor of Blairerno House, who stated in the petition that the 'wife [i.e. of Charles was] at present travelling, and [her] new address is unknown'.

On the same form a 'Statement of Particulars' gave such details as Charles's age, mental state, marital status, former occupation, religion and the ailment from which he was suffering – in this case, dipsomania brought on by drink. Curiously, however, the place cited on the statement as to where Charles was 'found and examined', was not Blairerno House but Newmill, Drumlithie, a hamlet situated half a mile or so to the east.[4]

Thirdly, two medical certificates were required, in which, 'a statement of facts indicative of insanity' was recorded. Medical Certificate No.1 was signed by Dr James Ironside (parochial medical officer for the adjacent parishes of Laurencekirk, Garvock and St Cyrus) who under the heading 'Facts indicating insanity observed by myself', wrote as follows:

> He [Charles] said he was to go away tonight [as] this was his last night [and] he had a message from God that he must go. He said he was getting messages from the unseen world, etc. Mr and Mrs Milne told me he had broken a whole window, then tried to run away. Then on being taken [apprehended] he struck every one he could get near.

Medical Certificate No.2 was signed by Dr James Duffus (parochial medical officer for Fordoun, Glenbervie and Fettercairn) who under the same heading said of Charles, 'He commenced to swear when I questioned him, and said that we were all a lot of devils. He afterwards refused to speak and also to move. Mr Forbes informed me that he smashed a window and Mr Milne said that he had kicked him.'[5]

Fourthly, a 'Certificate of Emergency', signed by Dr James Ironside confirmed that Charles Doyle 'is of unsound mind and a proper Patient to be placed in an asylum'. 'I the undersigned … hereby certify, on soul and conscience, that I have this day, at New Mill, (spelt sometimes as one word) Drumlithie in the County of Kincardine, seen and personally examined Charles Doyle … ' he wrote.[6]

Finally, a 'Reception Order', duly signed by the Sheriff, ordered the 'Transmission of the Lunatic [to the asylum]'.[7]

So what was Charles doing at New Mill, and who were Mr and Mrs Milne?

According to the census of 1881, the hamlet of Newmill consisted of the Mill of Newmill (occupied by miller and crofter Alexander Carnegie); Newmill Cottar House (occupied by an agricultural labourer and his family); Newmill (House), occupied by James Milne, aged thirty-nine, farmer of 140 acres, his wife Emily, their three children and three servants. A visiting clergyman was also present at that time, but no one else.

The declaration by Mr and Mrs Milne to the effect that Charles had, 'broken a whole window, then tried to run away', indicates that the latter may have been resident at New Mill for some time. Is it possible, that with the increasing numbers of boarders at Blairerno House, New Mill was used some time after 1881 for overspill and that some boarders were also looked after here by the farmer and his wife? (The fact that Blairerno House was an increasingly growing concern is born out by the fact that shortly after Charles Doyle left in May 1885, David Forbes, his family and the boarders moved to larger premises at Elsick House, Cookney, near Stonehaven, as further advertisements by him for the home in the *Medical Directory* indicate.)[8] New Mill was also convenient for visitors (including the doctors who came to examine Charles) in this pre-motor car era, Carmont station, on the main Dundee to Aberdeen railway line, being on site.

★   ★   ★

## MONTROSE ROYAL ASYLUM ('SUNNYSIDE' WING), 1885-1892

On 26 May 1885, Charles was duly admitted as a private patient to the 'Sunnyside' wing of the Montrose Royal Asylum, Scotland's oldest public asylum which at that time:

> ... housed some 500 inmates, of whom about 80 were private and the remainder pauper patients. The physician superintendent was Dr James Howden, who took up his post in 1858 and remained for the next forty years. In his annual reports he stated his credo: 'we must not ... lose sight of the great principle of non-restraint established by Pinel [Philippe, French physician, and pioneer of psychiatry], Tuke [William, Quaker philanthropist], Hill [Alsager Hay, social reformer], Connolly [John, innovator in the treatment of the mentally ill], and others, which have revolutionised the treatment of the insane, so that

the modern asylum has the character and aims of a Hospital and a Sanatorium rather than of a Prison or a Poorhouse'.

Like all public asylums, Montrose was inspected ever year by the Scottish Commissioners in Lunacy. Their reports consistently praised the work of the asylum, commended the humanity of the staff as well as the degree of liberty allowed to patients.[9]

At Montrose, Charles was described in the case notes on the day of his admission as being 'dangerous' but 'not epileptic' and 'not suicidal'. His 'Length of time [as being] Insane' was given as 'one day'.[10] Charles, it was stated:

Has been weak-minded and nervous from his youth, and from his own account, took refuge in alcoholics [i.e. alcoholic beverages] very early to give him courage. He was, 'calm on admission but very confused and bewildered ... his memory for recent events especially being very treacherous or altogether wanting. Bodily condition good.

It was also noted that Charles's attempted break out (from Blairerno House) occurred after 'he managed to procure drink ... .' The records continue:

1885. November 16. This morning had an epileptic attack of general convulsions, the first we have known him to have. He was very stupid for some hours afterwards, but did not know he had had a fit.

1886. May 28. Still confused and dazed. Tells me he made an attack on the servant girl, when he was the worst for drink.

June 3. Going on well, much less confused, is cheerful and happy and spends much of his time drawing.

July 14. During last week has been very queer; complained at first of great languor, then of an overpowering presentiment that he was going to die, that he would die in 48 hours; he was not in the least depressed at the thought but he took refuge in his prayer book, and had two long audiences with a priest, and prayed frequently.

November 16. Keeps much the same, often hypochondriacal, thinking he's dying.

1887. October 6. ... said he had seen his wife in the grounds and had a long conversation with her – which was pure fabrication.

October 23. Dull at present, filled with misgivings.

1888. March 23. Spends fully one half the day in prayer, sometimes kneeling in the billiard room with his prayer book – has no memory for anything recent but remembers well things he learnt and people he knew years ago.

November 1. Has often been in querulous humoures ... [and was still suffering from] ... delusions about his going to die soon.

1889. June 9. Having severe fits and had nine in all during the 24 hours.

June 14. Very confused and sometimes has talked absolute nonsense. On one occasion he got very excited and said that he was in hell and that the people round him were devils.[11]

★ ★ ★

So much for the medical profession's account of Charles. But how did *he* express himself? What were *his* thoughts, other than those which have already been described? This would have remained a mystery but for an extraordinary discovery made in the year 1977.

# Charles Doyle's Diary

In the year 1977, a book entitled *Charles Altimonte Doyle, His Diary, 8 March 1889*, came to light, written and illustrated by Charles while he was in Montrose Royal Asylum, Sunnyside Wing, in the year 1889 [Altimonte being the way he spelt his name, rather than Altamont, as it is commonly spelt].

A painting by him depicts the asylum as it was on 4 July 1889. 'Sunnyside picnic, 6th June 1889 and any nicer sandwiches and beer I never met …' is the caption for his sketch of the inmates of the asylum, seated on a bank enjoying a country scene. (The fact that beer was apparently offered to him is curious, bearing in mind that he was a confirmed alcoholic; or was this simply wishful thinking on his part?)

A decorative flower has the caption 'In Centre of Dining Table at Sunnyside – what delicious Soups this recals [sic] to My Memory'. Large birds, ducks, squirrels, flowers, trees and flowering fronds figure prominently. Why? Presumably because at 'Sunnyside', set as it was in extensive grounds in the middle of rolling countryside, there would have been flora and fauna all around him.

Many of his illustrations are of a cartoon-like character, where he often makes plays on words. For example, 'Who knows what a feature of golf this would be?' refers to a man attempting to hit a golf ball with his nose which is very long and shaped like a golf club. 'A new branch of hairdressing' depicts a young lady with a sprig of fern replacing a feather attached to her hair. True, there is the occasional, rather frightening image such as a sphinx with Charles in its mouth and the caption, 'Horrible phase of the artist worried by a sphinx'. But beside this are written the humorous words,

'Note, when I was drawing The Royal Institution, Edinburgh, I was a good deal worried by sphinxes.' An enormous squirrel nurses a baby, and Charles, with his caption, invites the reader to decide for himself whether, 'either this is a precious small Babe or a monstrous big Squirrel'.

Some of Charles's illustrations appear to reveal a caring side to his nature. For example, in 'An angel taking a soul to heaven', the soul appears to be that of a baby which the angel is cradling. A girl reproves an enormous bird – while at the same time shielding a butterfly from it behind her back.

Charles clearly has an eye for a pretty girl, of which there were evidently several on the large staff which that institution would have maintained. They are shown carrying fronds of foliage, dallying behind exotic plants, and sometimes coyly peeping out from between their leaves. Others hitch-hike on the backs of enormous birds, perhaps reflecting Charles's love of, and desire for freedom.

An expert on heraldry, which is his passion, Charles demonstrates his sense of humour by reproducing the Royal Coat of Arms with his own witty caption replacing the Latin words normally inscribed upon it. He again displays his knowledge, when beneath a drawing of a wild flower, he writes, 'These leaves are much used in Gothic stained glass.'

Charles is ever conscious of his Irish origins. 'What an Irishman was and is always believed to be under British rule' depicts a somewhat grizzled, downtrodden, ruffian-like figure, whereas 'What the Irishman certainly is under American rule' depicts a smart figure, attired in a suit and bearing an umbrella. Underneath Doyle writes, 'Tell us the reason why!'

Charles is immensely frustrated that his talents have not been recognised:

I am certain if my many VOLS of, well, I'll say of not serious work, were organised into some form submittable to the Public, they would tickle the taste of innumerable men like myself and be the source of much money which I should like to bestow on my Daughters, but imprisoned under most depressing restrictions what can I do? I believe I am branded as Mad, solely from the narrow Scotch Misconception of jokes … My claim for Sanity is not best made by Enlarging on my common sence [his spelling] – as in the possession of a Certain Class of ability demonstrated in this Book and proved by 30 years of Official Public Life, tho' unfortunately not seen by certain members of my own family – I would thought, however, that it would be the duty no less than the pleasure of refined Professional Gentlemen to protect men like myself – than otherwise – and not endorse utterly false conceptions of sanity or Insanity to the detriment of the life and liberty of a heartless gentleman ....

Nevertheless, Charles shows a certain amount of insight into his own shortcomings, for example, with, 'Back view of a frog's head', when he declares, 'It is judicious to hide it [the head] behind the flower. Would I could hide my other deficiencies!' And again, in a depiction of a woman scrubbing the floor with scrubbing brush, where the caption reads, 'Don't I wish I could clense [his spelling] my ways as she does hers soapeariorly [his play on words]'

On 22 May 1889, Charles writes:

I am not well. I will put off writing what I was going to say till tomorrow. What I wanted to say was that I had now done [produced] a great many Vols. Of ideas – but I am kept ignorant of what becomes of them. I asked [for] them to be all sent to Mrs Doyle [his wife Mary] and submitted to publishers, but as I have never had a single Book or Drawing acknowledged by her or other relatives I can only conclude that they see no profit in them. In these circumstances I think it would be better that these books should be entrusted to the Lunacy commissioners to show them the sort of Intellect they think it right to Imprison as Mad & let them judge if there is any question for publication.

He requests of the authorities:

That my two little Sketch Books might be sent to my poor dear wife Mary – not on account of their worth but just to show who I was thinking of, and besides there are lots of ideas in them which under professional advise [his spelling] might be utilised – that's all I've got to say – except God Bless her & the rest of them – who I dare say all forget me now – I don't them ....

In a poignant entry, Charles wistfully remembers his home and family:

I should like to mention one point on the inner-life of the Doyle Family when this Journal was written. – It is this – on Sunday the Day was observed by all the Children – Great and Small [i.e.

himself and his siblings] – Annette, James, Dick, Henry, Frank, Adelaide and myself going to the Mass celebrated at the French Chapel at eight o'clock A.M. This in Winter meant going from Cambridge Terrace, up Edgware Road, down George Street a Couple of Miles – often in the dark, and getting home to Breakfast at 10 – the after day was spent in perfect quiet till 8 in the Evening when the camphore Lamp and Mole Candles were lit in the Drawing Room, and guests began to arrive, often comprising the most distinguished Literary and Artistic Men of London, and Foreigners – [William Makepeace] Thackeray [English novelist] and Lover [presumably mistress] – [Samuel] Rothwell [Irish writer, artist, and songwriter] and Moor [English potter] … amongst others – Most delicious Music was discoursed by Annette on the piano – and James on the violoncello till about 10 when the Supper Tray was laid – generally just Cold Meats and Salad, followed by Punch.

This account was no flight of fancy on Charles's part, his son Arthur (Doyle) attesting to the fact that when his grandfather John's 'grand London friends passed through Edinburgh, they used … to call at the little flat,' and that he himself had once sat on the knee of the great William Thackeray.[1]

Charles then describes how 'we boys' all retired to bed at this point, where they discussed politics:

At this time I heard such horrible details of the passing of the Union between England and Ireland in 1788 at the Vote for which only Orangemen were admitted – that in itself makes the present Union quite <u>Illegal</u>'. Doyle then suggests that the best recourse would be for the Queen (Victoria) to 'call a parliament of Her Irish Subjects in Dublin – to legally Vote a Union if they think wise after due Debate – or Continue to sit in that City with the success – and prosperity which distinguished the former Parliaments held there.'[2]

Thoughts of death are often in Charles's mind. For instance, in 'Well met', a man with a beard, presumably Charles himself, shakes hands with a skeleton wielding a scythe. When Charles is lifted skywards by an angel, the caption reads simply, 'Being taken up'; and when he warmly embraces a skeleton, the caption reads, 'The close embrace'.

'Mary, my ideal home ruler' is a pun on the movement demanding home rule for Ireland, and depicts Charles sitting next to his wife (Mary) who is doing her sewing. A portrait of Charles, sitting with a kitten on his shoulders, bears another poignant caption, 'Where pussy used to sit at home. Observe her critical look, friendly but sorrowful.' On p.72, he writes, 'If this night 7th June should be my last – then my last expressed wish is God Bless my Wife Mary and my dear Children. Charles Altimonte Doyle.'

The impression given of himself by Charles in his diary is that of an accomplished and educated person, a fine draughtsman with beautiful handwriting and a great sense of humour, who is fascinated by making plays on words and whose amusing cartoons reflect his keen and dry sense of humour. Also, that he is well looked after at Sunnyside, where he enjoys his food. Etiquette is important to him even in the surroundings of the asylum, as is demonstrated in a delightful cameo sketch showing himself and another inmate of 'Sunnyside' greeting each other, with the caption, 'The amenities of polite society as every morning conducted in the dormitory of Sunnyside between Mr Frederick and his most obedient servant [i.e. Doyle].

The diary also reveals that Charles is from a household where music and literature are cherished, and one to which some of the most famous literati of the day were wont to call. His writings, particularly on the Irish question, show him to be a man of reason who also has a knowledge of history. Charles is someone who sees beauty all around him, and reflects this in his colourful and imaginative paintings. This is not to say that he is unaware of death, a subject which, with time on his hands, he often thinks about. Nonetheless, as a Roman Catholic he is confident that he will one day be borne up to Heaven by an angel, such as the one he portrays on p.60. Above all, he shows himself to be a very human person, who loves his wife and family and thinks of them often, and yet doubts if they ever think of him.

As Charles tries to keep cheerful and retain some semblance of dignity, deep down he harbours a bitter resentment that he, a gentleman, is being incarcerated for reasons which he cannot fully understand and for which, to some extent, he blames his family, although he is not unaware of his own shortcomings. He longs to escape from his confinement and sometimes even imagines that he has managed to do so. His diary is his statement of defiance to the world. 'Look what I can do!' he appears to be saying. 'How could a madman produce work as well-crafted, witty, and entertaining as this?' So *is* Charles in fact perfectly sane, and *has* he been incarcerated unjustly?

★ ★ ★

There is no doubt that it was the opinion of his wife Mary and that of the medical profession, that if Charles were to be released, he would immediately revert to drink, with disastrous consequences for both himself and his family. But are there any indications that he was actually insane?

Despite the obvious humour and *joie de vivre* in the diary's cartoons, there is the occasional pointer that all may not have been well in Charles's mind. His preoccupation with fairies and elf-like creatures (as depicted in 'The fairy cribbage table', and 'Fairy's nest in a flower pot') may perhaps be considered nothing unusual in one with an Irish background. But did Charles *actually believe* in fairies (as his son Arthur professed to do, thirty-three years later in 1922)?

The caption for an illustration of a chestnut branch in bud is, 'What a gush of matter into life is here', followed by the strange words, 'I have seen a green lad just like it.' Could this be a reference to 'little green men', a term which refers to extra-terrestrial humanoid-like beings with green skins and antennae? Equally strange is the depiction on p.28 of a girl whose features resemble that of a cat. Under the caption, 'Is this a girl or a cat? Or both?', Charles has written the curious words, 'I have known such a creature.'

Charles's comparing of a budding chestnut to a green lad may perhaps be dismissed simply as an illusion, this being defined as the misinterpretation of a real stimulus. However, his seeming preoccupation with fairies and his confusion between what is a girl and what is a cat suggests that he may also have been experiencing hallucinations, defined as perceptions that occur when there is no external stimulus. (It should be noted that vivid hallucinations are a feature of delirium tremens: a condition which may occur following the withdrawal of alcohol from a chronic alcoholic. In such cases, however, the hallucinations usually subside within a few days). The contents of a *visual hallucination* 'may appear normal or abnormal in size.'[3] This immediately brings to mind those illustrations in Charles's diary where many of the animals, plants and creatures illustrated by him are of hugely disproportionate size.

If these remarks in respect of Charles should appear fanciful, it should be noted that the doctors who treated him also diagnosed that he suffered from hallucinations, as will now be seen.

Apart from writing and illustrating his diary, it would appear that whilst at Montrose, Charles prepared the illustrations for *Remollescences of a Medical Student* by J.A. Sidney (1886), and of course *A Study in Scarlet* by his son Doyle (1887–88).

# From Montrose to Edinburgh and Dumfries

Charles's case notes for his time spent at the Montrose Royal Asylum indicate a remorseless deterioration in his condition: '1891. January 5. Has occasional attacks of entire mental aberration. At others [times] is a most interesting person to talk to.' On 14 January 1892, Doctor James Howden, Physician Superintendent at Montrose (1858-1898) examined Charles and declared him to be, 'subject to attacks of depression when he has groundless fears as to his physical and spiritual condition.'[1] Dr Grealbalch of Montrose described Charles's 'usual mental state' during his time at Sunnyside as being:

> ... one of passive contentment with entire loss of memory for recent events. He is an artist of some ability, and when in this condition spends the whole day sketching. He is, however, subject to fits of listlessness and excitement which occur at intervals of about a month usually, where he has hallucinations of hearing and sight and is then a source of some trouble. This condition rarely lasts for more than a day or two and he has no recollection of it afterwards. Mr Doyle takes [epileptic] fits usually about every month or six weeks. In the interval he is quite free from them, but usually has two or three severe fits in one day. Twice he has been on the verge of status epilepticus [prolonged and repeated epileptic fits without intervening recovery of consciousness, which may prove fatal] on these occasions.[2]

During his time at Montrose, Charles had fits on a continuing basis: sometimes as many as seven in one month. The only treatment given was potassium bromide and on 14 June 1889, a glass of whisky, morning and evening, which seems illogical considering that he had been diagnosed as a dipsomaniac![3]

Despite his various afflictions, Charles contributed various articles and cartoons to the *Sunnyside Chronicle* [an in-house magazine for the 'Sunnyside' wing of the asylum, which was produced between 1781-1981].[4]

## THE ROYAL EDINBURGH ASYLUM, JANUARY TO MAY 1892

On 23 January 1892, Charles was transferred from Montrose to the above institution on the authority of the Board of Lunacy 'as an ordinary patient and boarder', for the fee of £42 per annum (the document of transfer having been signed by his wife Mary). His bodily condition was 'weak', and he was said to be suffering from 'epileptic dementia'.

The Royal Edinburgh Asylum which was designed by Robert Reid opened in 1813 and was described as 'a grim, grey building in 4 acres of grounds, surrounded by high walls.' There was a 'curling pond' in the grounds where, in winter, able bodied inmates could participate in the game of 'curling', which was popular in Scotland and consisted in rolling heavy, smooth, round stones across a sheet if ice.

It was not until 1840 that the first physician superintendent Dr William McKirnon of Aberdeen was appointed. Under his aegis, patients were taught carpentry, tailoring, shoe-making, basket-making, book-binding, and printing, with gardening and pig-keeping being offered as outdoor occupations. Another innovation was for a former schoolmaster to be brought in to teach those patients who were illiterate. Jane Upton McDougall's appointment as matron coincided with Dr McKirnon's arrival. The former was the first matron 'with any semblance of real nursing experience behind her.'[5]

In that same year, plans were submitted by architect William Burn, for a new three-storey asylum, subsequently known as 'West House' (the original building, subsequently known as 'East House', being reserved for fee-paying patients). West House, which was not fully completed until the 1860s, was laid out in the shape of a letter 'H' and consisted of workrooms, dayrooms, bathrooms, sickrooms, dormitories, a room for 'dirty' patients and 'cells' for 'noisy patients'. The presence of iron grilles of similar pattern behind many of the 'small-pane sashes' (sash windows) indicate that for some of the patients, at any rate, this was a secure establishment from which they were not intended to stray![6] The 'airing galleries' on the upper levels were presumably where patients were permitted to take the air. At the rear were the kitchen and dining hall. Separate from this were the laundry, the hospital, and a house for 'refractory patients'.

When, in 1846, Dr McKirnon retired, he was succeeded by Dr David Skae who instigated clinical lectures in psychiatry at the asylum. At the time of Charles Doyle's admission in January 1892, the physician superintendent was Dr Thomas Smith Clouston.

Charles Doyle's notes from his time at the Royal Edinburgh Asylum are still extant; being kept in the 'West House' casebook – indicating that this is where he was incarcerated. So why, as a fee-paying patient, did he not reside at East House? The answer is that in West House's four accommodation blocks, patients were divided into the following categories and strictly segregated from one another: male paupers, female paupers, male upper class patients and female upper class patients. In other words, Charles was classified as an 'upper class patient' who could afford to pay intermediate-level fees but not in the same league as those who could afford to pay the fees of the more luxurious East House!

In the words of Harriet Richardson, 'The Enlightenment which took place in the latter part of the eighteenth century produced a more humanitarian attitude to the conditions of the insane.'[7] The names Alsager Hay Hill, John Connolly, William Tuke and Philippe Pinel have already been mentioned in relation to the Montrose Royal Asylum, and it appears that Pinel (1745–1826) may have influenced the ethos of the Royal Edinburgh Asylum also, as evidenced by the 'Mask of Pinel': a bust of his face which appears on the arch above the original entrance. So how had this come about?

Born in 1745, Philippe Pinel was the son of a barber surgeon from the village of St Paul near Toulouse, from which university he graduated in medicine. He subsequently moved to Paris where he met:

> many of the men who were playing a part in the great movement out
> of which came the French Revolution. In that movement was a general
> movement for the betterment of humanity … . Questions of teaching,
> education, hospitals, and the treatment of the insane – all these were
> being discussed. Thus, when the Revolution broke out in 1789, a good
> many solutions of these questions had already been prepared.[8]

In 1793, Pinel became physician at the Bicêtre Hospital in Paris, where of the 4,000 or so male patients, about 200 were mentally ill. 'At this very moment,

[Georges] Couthon, one of the bloodthirsty ringleaders of the Reign of Terror, gave his sanction to Pinel to begin his humane reforms.' Pinel responded by striking off the chains by which fifty-three of his patients were bound and abolishing the traditional therapies of purging, bleeding and blistering.[9] From henceforth, the reforms which he instigated, 'included everything that could ameliorate the condition of the insane, such as [providing] suitable building, warm clothing, good food, and the comforts of life. He also introduced careful medical examination.'[10] (In this same year, the French revolutionaries sent King Louis XVI and his Queen, Marie Antoinette, to the guillotine, Pinel being a reluctant witness to the former event).

In 1795, Pinel became chief physician at the city's Hospice de la Salpêtrière for Women and was appointed Professor of Medical Pathology. In 1801, Pinel's book *Traité médico-philosophique sur l'alienation mentale (Medico-Philosophical Treatise on Mental Alienation or mania) was* published, and translated into English by D.D. Davis as *A Treatise on Insanity*.

The connection between Pinel and Edinburgh arose by virtue of the fact that:

After the termination of the Napoleonic wars (1800–1801), young medical men from Edinburgh University were attracted to Paris by the fame of its medical school. Among these young men were Sir Robert Christison, the famous Professor of Medical Jurisprudence, and Dr Andrew Combe, the physiologist and phrenologist. They attended the lectures on mental diseases delivered at the Salpêtrière by Esquirol, the friend and pupil of Pinel. They met Pinel in the wards of the hospital and heard all about his great reforms. Twenty years afterwards these two men were elected managers of the Edinburgh hospital. About this time it was decided to enlarge the hospital, and when the West House was designed a bust of Pinel was placed over the entrance archway. It was interesting to note that this was the first memorial to be erected to the memory of Pinel and his work; for the French did not erect a statue till 1885.[11]

★ ★ ★

Charles's case notes for the time he spent at The Royal Edinburgh Asylum do not make for encouraging reading; for despite the best efforts of the staff, he continued to deteriorate:

17 February 1892: Mr Doyle is an illustrative alcoholic case, both physically and mentally. His memory is much impaired. His lack of initiative is very marked. He has numerous hallucinations of hearing, saying that his children are speaking to him. His religious emotions are strong and he spends a great deal of the day reading religious books. Last night at ten o'clock he had the first fit he has had since admission, and he had a second this forenoon. They were not severe, however, lasting only a minute or so. He did not know he had had any fit but said he thought he might have had one from the feeling of exhaustion.

7 May 1892: He is very thin and run-down. He takes slight fits often. His pulse is very weak. He walks in the garden of the hospital, is very religious and reads his Bible a lot.[12]

When Charles was discharged on 31 May 1892, his condition was said to be 'not improved'.

## CRICHTON ROYAL HOSPITAL, DUMFRIES, MAY 1892 TO OCTOBER 1893

On 31 May 1892, Charles, now aged sixty, was transferred from the Royal Edinburgh Asylum to the above institution, again as a private patient. According to the medical case notes he had been diagnosed with dipsomania but was 'certainly not dangerous to others.' Under the subheading, 'Family known to be, or to have been insane' the answer given was 'No'. He was 'Mildly depressed. Enfeeblement was marked: is facile and childish.' His memory was said to be 'bad' and he was suffering from 'dementia'. General bodily health and condition were 'weak'. However, during what were to be the last months of his life, Charles appears to have been reasonably contented apart from suffering from the epilepsy which had dogged him through the years:

1.6.[18]92: 'Mr Doyle slept well last night and is taking food well. His memory is very defective. E.g. he cannot remember faces. Forgets that he has been visited by doctor in the morning.'

2.6.92: 'He is perfectly happy, says everything is splendid, that he has slept so well, and had so good a breakfast. When indoors he spends his time in reading books and newspapers. Goes out walking and driving [presumably in a pony trap].'

21.6.92: 'Mr Doyle had an ordinary epileptic fit today.'

4.8.92: 'Mr Doyle had an epileptic fit this morning.' [The notes then leap forward a year].

4.8.93: 'Very feeble, restless and noisy. Quite incoherent in conversation.'

25.9.93: 'Got up today for first time for months. Is rather more sensible.'

3.10.93: 'Pleasant and easily pleased. Solemnly presented me with an empty paper which he assured me contained gold dust and was a reward for professional attendance. He said he had collected it in the moonlight on the bed.'

10.10.93: 'Died in a fit during the night.'[13]

Charles, who had died at the age of sixty-one, is buried at High Cemetery, Craig Road, Dumfries. The inscription on his gravestone is from the biblical *Book of Solomon*: 'Until the day break and the shadows flee away'. Interred with him are his three elder daughters: Annette, Katherine and Mary.

* * *

Whether the family visited Charles during his long years spent in various asylums is not known, but it would seem unlikely. However, to the credit of his wife Mary, she did what she could to help given her straitened circumstances, as her letter sent from Masongill Cottage on 3 December 1892 to Dr James Rutherford, Physician Superintendent at Crichton Royal Hospital, reveals:

I am extremely sorry you were troubled about that suit of clothes. For years we have sent my husband things of our eldest son's [Arthur] (always as good as new) as they are much of a size. By an inadvertence, this time they were sent direct from the cleaner's, instead of through our tailors, who would have out right the matter you allude to. The buttons were taken off to have new ones put [on]. Mr. Doyle can have a suit made for him or his measures [measurements] sent to me and I can supply one. But the prices must be reasonable. My means are so very small that I live in a cottage at £8 a year and keep no servant![14]

Charles's faults did not prevent his son from recognising and appreciating his talents as an artist, so much so that in 1888, Doyle invited Charles to provide six pen-and-ink drawings for the Ward Lock edition of *A Study in Scarlet*, the first full-length novel featuring Sherlock Holmes.[15] Doyle also hung several of Charles's pictures on the walls of his study and drawing room.[16]

Another measure of Doyle's appreciation of his father's abilities is reflected in the fact that in the year 1924, Doyle exhibited some fifty of Charles's works at an exhibition in London, declaring that:

> ... his work had a very peculiar style of its own, mitigated by great natural humour. He was more terrible than [William] Blake [English painter, poet, engraver, and mystic] and less morbid than [Anton Joseph] Wiertz [Belgian painter]. His originality is best shown by the fact that one hardly knows with whom to compare him.[17]

In Doyle's autobiography he described his father as 'far the greatest ... of the family', as far as being an artist was concerned:

> My father's life was full of the tragedy of unfulfilled powers and of undeveloped gifts. He had his weaknesses, as all of us have ours, but he had also some very remarkable and outstanding virtues.... I am sure that Charles Doyle had no enemy in the world, and that those who knew him best sympathized most with the hard fate which had thrown him, a man of sensitive genius, into an environment which neither his age nor his nature were fitted to face.[18]

## 23

# Charles Doyle: Towards a Diagnosis

By examining the information provided by the aforementioned institutions in which Charles spent the last fourteen years of his life, is it possible, with modern knowledge, to achieve a greater understanding of his mental condition than was possible at the time? And if so, does this in turn shed light on the apparent mental aberrations which his son Arthur (Doyle), showed in his latter years?

In the early years of Charles's illness the problem was to determine whether his abnormal behaviour was caused by alcohol or by some inherent defect in his personality. A similar problem would arise in his latter years when the symptoms of epilepsy, and later of dementia, would be additional complicating factors.

## DEMENTIA

Defined as a general decline in all areas of mental ability, dementia can cause 'behavioural, affective, and psychotic features …', to occur.[1] In fact, Charles suffered from pre-senile dementia, or Alzheimer's Disease, which occurs prior to the age of sixty-five and is often characterised by delusions and hallucinations.[2] However, the earliest mention of Charles having dementia was not until 23 January 1892 when he was aged sixty and in the penultimate year of his life.

## Epilepsy

A likely explanation for Charles's epilepsy and consequent seizures may lie in the following statement:

> A 'binge' on alcohol can cause a seizure, even in people who do not have epilepsy. Such seizures can be due to alcohol withdrawal, toxic effects of alcohol, too much fluid, metabolic changes in the body and vitamin or nutritional deficiencies. Studies suggest that alcohol withdrawal seizures usually happen 7-48 hours after reducing or stopping excessive or prolonged alcohol intake.
>
> Some people who continue to drink large quantities of alcohol and who experience further seizures are quite likely to develop epilepsy as a result of this. Even if alcohol consumption is stopped altogether, the seizures may continue to happen unless anti-epileptic medication is introduced and seizure control gained.[3]

Therefore, the likelihood is that Charles's epilepsy was the result of his drinking and that the symptoms of that epilepsy continued, in the absence of any effective treatment, for the rest of his life. And this, despite the fact that drink was largely withheld from him, which as shown, is often the case in such circumstances.

## Epilepsy and Psychosis

A person suffering from epilepsy may, in consequence, also suffer from various types of psychiatric disorder, including, '… cognitive, affective [mood], emotional, and behavioural disturbances. These can occur before, during, after, or between seizures. The evidence supports the view that epilepsy is associated with an increased risk of psychosis, especially, but not exclusively schizophrenia-like in presentation.'[4] During the period between epileptic seizures, '… religious and paranoid delusions appear to be particularly common… .'[5] (A delusion is defined as a fixed, irrational idea not shared by others and not responding to reasoned argument.)

So can Charles's psychiatric problems be attributed solely to his epilepsy? The only way to answer this question is to ascertain what his mental state was like *before his epilepsy overtook him and thereby clouded the picture.*

On Charles's admission to the Montrose Royal Asylum on 26 May 1885, it was specifically stated in his hospital case notes that he was 'not epileptic'. In fact, his first epileptic fit occurred six months later on 16 November of that year.

## CHARLES PRIOR TO 16 NOVEMBER 1885

Charles's attempt to break out of New Mill on 26 May 1885 may simply have been the result of intense frustration at being incarcerated; the violence used being attributable to the alcohol which he is known to have acquired on that occasion (hence the expression 'fighting drunk'). On the other hand, Dr James Ironside, who examined Charles on that date and certified him as being insane, stated that Charles had told him that he had received '*a message from God that he must go*' [which could mean either leave New Mill, or depart this life], and that Charles had also, 'said he was *getting messages from the unseen world*.' So, suddenly, here is a snippet of first-hand information, which not only confirms that Charles was hearing voices – which is indicative of a *serious and inherent psychiatric disorder*, but which also is instantly reminiscent of the spiritualistic experiences that his son (Doyle) would describe in his later life.

(Of course, after Charles's first epileptic fit on 16 November 1885, it is impossible to say which of his hallucinations and delusions were caused by epilepsy and which were caused by this inherent mental disorder. These include the hallucinations which he evidently experienced in the year 1889 when he was writing his diary; the strong and persistent belief that he was shortly going to die; that he was in hell and that the people around him were devils; that his children were speaking to him; that he had seen his wife in the grounds of the Montrose asylum, and had held a conversation with her). So what might this inherent mental illness have been?

★　★　★

Charles's predominant symptoms, *hallucinations and delusions*, are common in two diseases: schizophrenia and bipolar disorder (the latter being characterised by mania – or elevation of mood, alternating with depression).

## Bipolar Disorder

Depression, which Charles is reported to have suffered from frequently, is a feature of bipolar disorder as are his 'fits of listlessness and excitement.'

## Acute Schizophrenia

In the acute phase of this disease the sufferer may display a pre-occupation with his or her religion (which was true of Charles), or show an intense interest in other phenomena (in Charles's case, gnomes, fairies and the like). Auditory hallucinations are common (those experienced by Charles being of an informative nature, or making predictions about his future).

Over-activity and disturbances of behaviour are common in schizophrenia and although major violence towards others is not common, it certainly does occur. For example, Humphries and Johnstone (1992), found that in a group of 253 patients with a first schizophrenic episode, 52 behaved in a way threatening to the lives of others. In about half the patients, the behaviour was directly attributable to psychotic symptoms, usually delusions.

Threats of violence should be taken seriously, particularly if there is a history of such behaviour in the past, regardless of whether the patient was ill at the time. The danger usually resolves as acute symptoms are brought under control but a few patients pose a continuing threat.[6]

So although Charles's violent outbursts have been attributed to his drinking, could schizophrenia also have been a factor in this?

It has to be said that in one respect, Charles was an atypical schizophrenic, in that he had a definite insight into his own condition (as his diary shows), which schizophrenics do not.

## Chronic Schizophrenia

This is characterised by intermittent under-activity, a lack of drive, social withdrawal and emotional apathy. Again, this does not appear to chime with the picture of Charles painted by his hospital records where he remains reasonably alert right up to the end.

## CONCLUSION

For the psychiatrist, it is convenient to try to make sense of human behaviour by looking for patterns whereby abnormalities can by classified as syndromes. However, because of the complexity of human experience, and perhaps more importantly because of what is now known about the infinite variability of the genetic code, it is not always possible to make a perfect match. In other words, a subject may display some but not all of the symptoms and signs required to fit the definition of one particular disease and there is frequently a degree of overlap with another. Charles is no exception to this rule and from his case notes it would appear that he displays some but not all of the characteristic symptoms of both bipolar disorder and schizophrenia. This fact is recognised in psychiatric circles, and a patient such as Charles, who displays traits characteristic of both bipolar disorder and schizophrenia, is said to be suffering from a *schizo-affective disorder* (the word affect meaning mood).

\*   \*   \*

Perhaps the most interesting question of all has to be, was Charles suffering from this schizo-affective disorder in his early years and even before he took to drink? Up until now, it has always been assumed that the drink caused the mental disorder. But was it the other way around and was it *because of the mental disorder that Charles turned to drink*? From the following statement, the answer would appear to be, yes:

> Alcohol misuse is commonly found in conjunction with other psychiatric disorders *and sometimes appears to be secondary to them*. For example, some patients with depressive disorders take to alcohol in the mistaken hope that it will alleviate low mood. Those with anxiety disorders, particularly panic disorder and social phobia, are also at risk. Alcohol misuse is also seen in patients with bipolar disorder [characterised by swings in moods to opposite extremes] and schizophrenia.[7]

The statement continues:

> … the management of patients with both substance misuse [in Charles's case, alcohol] and serious psychiatric illness such as schizophrenia

and bipolar disorder poses several additional challenges. Such co-morbidity is associated with an increased risk of violence and suicide. Patients with dual diagnoses are particularly hard to retain in treatment and frequently present in crisis with many unmet social needs.[8]

The inference is clear. From his early adult life, Charles suffered from a schizo-affective disorder which predisposed him to alcohol abuse, and of which the doctors who treated him at the time were unaware. In fact, it was a lay person – his wife Mary – who came closest to making the real diagnosis when in her letter to Dr James Rutherford, dated 3 December 1892, she described her husband Charles's condition as being 'a real madness'.[9]

# Doyle's Delusions: An Inherited Disease?

A s shown, Doyle experienced hallucinations and delusions, probably as a feature of an inherent tendency to mania. His father Charles suffered from a schizo-affective disorder causing him also to have hallucinations and delusions with occasional outbursts of violence. So were any other members of the family similarly affected?

Charles's brother Richard frequently attended séances held by spiritualists and was also enthusiastic about spirit photography.[1] Richard had more than a passing interest in fairies, elves, dragons, giants and the like, which was understandable for an imaginative person such as he: this being a time when fairy stories were much in vogue. He illustrated such volumes as *The Fairy Ring* (a collection of fairy tales by the Brothers Grimm), and *Fairy Tales from All Nations* by Anthony Whitehill and also wrote and illustrated fairy stories of his own. And was it not he who allegedly introduced his young nephew Doyle to this so-called 'other world'?

However, there are reasons for thinking that Richard's interest was perhaps more of an obsession. He visited Devon, where the Reverend Sabine Baring-Gould, writer, collector of legends, and rector of the village of Lewtrenchard, had publicly declared in his book *Curious Myths of the Middle Ages, 1866–68* that he himself had actually seen goblins. In Yorkshire, 'a well-known site of fairy sightings', Richard 'kept a close eye out for signs of his favourite subjects.'[2] Of his painting, *Elves Battling with Frogs*, Richard remarked, 'This event, it is supposed, took place in pre-historic times, or [i.e. otherwise] it might have been added to the fifteen decisive battles of the world – making sixteen.'[3] Was this written tongue-in-cheek or did he actually believe that such an event had really taken place? Richard was a devout Roman Catholic who had resigned, after a seven year period spent as illustrator for *Punch* magazine, in protest at its publication in 1850 of a series of cartoons ridiculing the Pope and Roman Catholicism. If he *did* believe in fairies and the like, then this would certainly have been at odds with his Catholic faith.

Although Richard's fairies are, in the main, beautiful and sensitively depicted, it has to be said that there is often a certain grotesqueness not only about some of his other creatures but also in the subject matter chosen: a giant with his murdered victims suspended from the belt around his waist; another who has fallen into a pit about to be slain by an elf wielding a pickaxe; his *Dragon of Wantley* belches fire over his victims and devours cattle and even children; his *Battle of Elves and Crows*, where the latter appear to be pecking the former to death, is even more disturbing.

Did Richard simply possess an over vivid imagination? Or did he *genuinely believe* in the 'other world' as described above. And if so, is he therefore to be described as insane? Where does the boundary of sanity finish and that of insanity begin? Did it ever occur to his contemporaries or to those who have written about him since that there was something slightly odd about Richard Doyle? Is it possible that he had some psychological problem similar in nature to that which afflicted his brother Charles and also, latterly, his nephew Doyle?

Although Doyle's daughter Mary managed her father's psychic bookshop in London, she said of spiritualism, 'I tried to go along with it, but couldn't.' However, she did admit to being 'drawn into a circle of teachers, using [i.e. who used] a medium to convey their ideas.' As time went by however, Mary's attitude changed in that she endorsed 'what Daddy had known all along – the great need which at that time existed and the help that many people could only get through spiritualism.'[4] Mary also stated that when visiting the USA she found she was one of the 'chosen ones' in her theosophical circle.[5] It appears therefore, that Mary was receptive to psychic phenomena as is apparent from her statement, 'The personal side of the psychic is true as long as it is conveyed to us [presumably by a medium]. *We must not try to search it out*',[6] but whether this extended to her having hallucinations and delusions is not known.

\* \* \*

Doyle was a qualified doctor and the possibility that his father's mental illness had a hereditary basis may well have crossed his mind. A clue that this may have been the case is contained in his fictional story *The Empty House*, where Sherlock Holmes alludes to the fact that his adversary, Colonel Sebastian Moran, ostensibly a pillar of the establishment, is suffering from a hereditary disease. First, Holmes checks Moran's details in his index of biographies:

> Born London, 1840. Son of Sir Augustus Moran, C.B., once British Minister to Persia. Educated Eton and Oxford. Served in Jowaki Campaign, Afghan Campaign, Charasiab (dispatches), Sherpur, and Cabul. Author of *Heavy Game of the Western Himalayas*, 1881; *Three Months in the Jungle*, 1884. Address: Conduit Street. Clubs: The Anglo-Indian, the Tankerville, the Bagatelle Card Club.

So what went wrong to make this once 'honourable soldier' (in Watson's words) become the 'bosom friend' of the evil Professor Moriarty, and in Holmes' opinion, 'the second most dangerous man in London?' Holmes explained it by making an analogy with nature:

> There are some trees, Watson, which grow to a certain height and then suddenly develop some unsightly eccentricity. You will see it often in humans. I have a theory that the individual represents in his development the whole procession of his ancestors, and that such a sudden turn to good or evil stands for some strong influence which came into the line of his pedigree. The person becomes, as it were, the epitome of the history of his own family.

As already mentioned, for the writer of fiction the temptation to include details of personal biography in his or her stories is often irresistible. So could it be that when Holmes suggests that the colonel's 'evil' mind was the result of a hereditary disease, Doyle was in fact *thinking of his own father Charles*?

★  ★  ★

Psychiatrists agree that there is a tendency for affective (mood) disorders and schizophrenia to be inherited, though the genetic mechanism for this has yet to be elucidated. A clue as to what may have occurred in the case of Doyle and his father Charles, is contained in the following statements:

[There is] … an average lifetime risk of about 5-10 per cent among first-degree relatives of schizophrenics [i.e. of inheriting schizophrenia], compared with 0.2-0.6 per cent among first-degree relatives of controls.[7]

At present it appears that the risk of delusional disorder is increased in first-degree relatives of patients with schizophrenia …'[8]

## CONCLUSION

While it is not suggested that Doyle was suffering from schizophrenia, the second statement suggests that he may well have inherited his delusional disorder from his father Charles (who had exhibited many of the features of a schizophrenic).

# Epilogue

Sir Arthur Conan Doyle died on 7 July 1930 aged seventy-one, at his home Windlesham, where his remains were interred in the garden. The following Sunday, a memorial service was held for him at London's Royal Albert Hall, organised by the Marylebone Spiritualist Association. His wife Jean died in 1940, and was buried beside him. In 1955 (Windlesham having previously been sold by the family), both bodies were exhumed and reburied at All Saints Church, Minstead not far from Bignell Wood, the Doyle's country retreat in Hampshire's New Forest.

Inscribed on Doyle's tombstone, which incidentally takes the form of a Christian cross, are the words: 'Knight. Patriot, physician and man of letters Steel true, blade straight.' (The last line being a quotation from a poem by Robert Louis Stevenson entitled *My Wife*).

Looking back over Doyle's life, it is difficult to see how anyone could have fitted more into it, unless of course they were superhuman! Medicine, writing, sport, politics, and latterly, the paranormal being subjects of consuming interest. In the typical British way he was strongly motivated to support the underdog. Above all, his quest was to discover the true meaning of human existence and more specifically, to overcome the seemingly insurmountable barrier between life and death. It is this that drove him onwards. It is as if he simply could not bear to accept the idea of death as meaning a final separation from loved ones.

His prodigious output of books has already been touched upon and his single-mindedness in producing them is illustrated by his son Adrian:

... before he wrote *The White Company*, he buried himself for a year in a tiny cottage in the New Forest, his sole companions being sixty-five works of reference on every aspect of the fourteenth century. Usually, he was at work in his study by 6.30 each morning, an hour's sleep in the afternoon, work until 11 at night, and then to bed with the Bible, a treatise on the latest excavations in Egypt or, perhaps, all the newspaper reports on the Heavyweight [boxing] Championship ... .

In *The Times*, at time of the South African War, he wrote, suggesting the formation of the Imperial Yeomanry ... . When Queen Victoria died, he wrote [again] to *The Times* advocating the change in the Coronation Oath which would delete the insult to Catholics. Before The Great War he saw exactly how Germany would use her submarines against our food carriers ..., and had a story [published] in The *Strand* [Magazine] to illustrate it, after sending memoranda, in vain, to the Navy and War Office.[1]

Adrian goes on to give an account of his father's sporting prowess, albeit a somewhat exaggerated one, which is nonetheless illustrative of the enormous energy and talent of a man who was burly, well built, over 6ft in height, and weighed in at about 15 stones:

I believe that I am correct in stating that Conan Doyle played for Hampshire in both football and cricket. He most certainly figured much in first-class cricket with the M.C.C.; reached the third round of the amateur billiards championship; was a hard rider to hounds; drove as one of the British team in the Prince Henry race against Germany [Prince Heinrich – 'Henry' – of Prussia, brother of Kaiser Wilhelm II, who loved to engage in motor sports]; introduced skiing into Switzerland [In fact, Doyle merely claimed that he had introduced skis into the Grisons division (canton) of Switzerland], and finally, was a dangerous man with the [boxing] gloves.[2]

Doyle's generosity was touched upon by his mother Mary, in a letter that she wrote in December 1892:

My son is very good and generous to us. He pays half of his brother's [Innes's] expenses at Woolwich [Army Academy], besides paying for one sister abroad at school and keeping two sisters living with him. He

has his own wife and children to maintain. I know he would help me
sooner than have his father out [i.e. released from the asylum].[3]

Of Doyle's patriotism and sense of duty there is no doubt, and yet having witnessed two wars at first hand he is quite sanguine when it comes
to the subject of international conflict. For example, in *The Adventure of
the Cardboard Box,* he describes (vicariously through his character Sherlock
Holmes), 'this method of settling international questions' – i.e. resorting to
war – as 'ridiculous'. Although this was a reference to the American Civil
War, Doyle no doubt intended the same sentiment to be applicable to
all wars.

Neither is he at all jingoistic when it comes to the subject of war, and
he was even respected by his former enemies the Boers, whom he had
encountered at first-hand in the South African War, as this account by his
son Adrian indicates:

> His (Doyle's) history *The Great Boer War* is still accepted as the classical
> account and was so fair in its contents that the most full and flattering
> review of it was written from St Helena by one of the Boer leaders
> extolling its impartial and chivalrous spirit.[4]

★　★　★

Despite Doyle being a high achiever in many different fields, it seems
highly likely that a man of his discernment and intuition would have
lived his life with the thought always in the back of his mind that one
day he might succumb to the same mental illness as his father Charles
had done. He would doubtless have been relieved to reach middle age
without such an untoward event occurring. However, when mental illness did finally overcome Doyle, he failed to recognise it; the
illness itself having nullified his ability to have insight into his own
condition.

With the death of Doyle, the trait of mental instability present in the
family that had affected both him, his father Charles, and possibly his uncle
Richard appears to have come to an end; although it has to be said that at
least two of his children, his first wife Louise's daughter Mary and his second wife Jean's son Denis, shared his psychic interests.[5] So what became of
his surviving family?

Of his siblings, Annette became a governess in Portugal, where she died in 1890; Lottie married Captain Leslie Oldham of the Royal Engineers, ho was killed in the First World War as already mentioned; Connie married journalist E.W. Hornung; Ida, following in Annette's footsteps, became a governess in Portugal and later married Nelson Foley, a distant relative and wealthy industrialist; Dodo married the Reverend Charles Cyril Angell.

Of Doyle's children by Louise, Mary managed his psychic bookshop in London, as already stated.[6] Of his children by Jean, Denis married a Russian princess and assisted Doyle with his spiritualist 'propaganda' work;[7] Adrian took a Danish wife and participated in motor racing and big game hunting, becoming a Fellow of the Zoological Society. He also added to his father's collection of Sherlock Holmes stories by writing several of his own. Jean became Air Commandant and Director of the Women's Royal Air Force.

Author Georgina Doyle states that neither Denis nor Adrian were '… trained to do any proper work. It seemed that his sons gradually dropped Arthur's spiritualist cause. Driving fast cars was a far more natural and enjoyable pursuit for young men.'

After his mother Jean's death in 1940, Adrian is said to have had 'some sort of nervous breakdown', and displayed 'subsequent erratic behaviour.'[8] Adrian's doctor described him as having 'an overanxious nature', with 'grand, unrealistic ideas about his capabilities.'[9] (This is reminiscent of the type of grandiose delusions suffered by Doyle himself).

★   ★   ★

In the final chapter of his autobiography entitled *The Psychic Quest*, Doyle anticipated the coming of a very different world, where:

> … the sources of all force would be traced rather to spiritual than to material causes.

> In religion one can perhaps see a little more clearly. Theology and dogma would disappear. People would realize that such questions as the number of persons in God, or the process of Christ's birth, have no bearing at all upon the development of man's spirit, which is the sole object of life.
> All religions would be equal, for all alike produce gentle, unselfish souls who are God's elect. Christian, Jew, Buddhist, and Mohammedan

would shed their distinctive doctrines, follow their own high teachers on a common path of morality, and forget all that antagonism which has made religion a curse rather than a blessing to the world.

We shall be in close touch with other-world forces, and knowledge will supersede that faith which has in the past planted a dozen different signposts to point in as many different directions.

Such will be the future, so far as I can dimly see it ...

Perhaps it should be left to Doyle's son Adrian to have the final word, with this description of his father, who, even in his latter years, was still living and enjoying life to the full:

In the most cavalier manner possible, [he, Doyle] would lose far more money than he could afford in support of every wild project of treasure trove or sunken galleon; the adventurer who in the last year of his life would insist that he should experience the sensation of 120 m.p.h. in the mechanic's seat of a racing car; the companion who strode across the moonlit moor holding forth in the most fascinating manner on the Weald strata or the bloody history of the Ashdown smugglers and roaring out sea chanties [shanties] in a manner that leaves memory behind it as fresh and as happy as the salt wind in one's face.[10]

# Notes

## Chapter 1: Formative Years and Influences

1. Doyle, Adrian Conan, *The True Conan Doyle*, p.6.
2. Doyle, Sir Arthur Conan, *Memories and Adventures*, p.2.
3. Nordon, Pierre, *Conan Doyle*, p.4.
4. Doyle, Adrian Conan, op.cit., p.6.
5. Doyle, Georgina, *Out of the Shadows*, pp.32,34,35.
6. Doyle, Sir Arthur Conan, *Memories and Adventures*, p.8.
7. Roden, Barbara, www.ash-tree.bc.ca/acdsfairies.htm 29/03/2006.
8. Glaister, John, *A Text-Book of Medical Jurisprudence and Toxicology*, p.607

## Chapter 2: From Doctor to Writer: Sherlock Holmes

1. Doyle, Sir Arthur Conan, *Memories and Adventures*, p.20.
2. Ibid, p.69.
3. Ibid, p.24.
4. Ibid, p.11.
5. Doyle, Georgina, *Out of the Shadows*, p.41.
6. Engen, Rodney, *Richard Doyle*, p.168.
7. Doyle, Sir Arthur Conan, op.cit., p.20.
8. Ibid, p.34.
9. Ibid, p.47.
10. Booth, Martin, *The Doctor, The Detective, and Arthur Conan Doyle*, p.103.
11. Doyle, Sir Arthur Conan, op.cit, p.79.
12. Stashower, Daniel, *Teller of Tales: The Life of Arthur Conan Doyle*, p.95.
13. Doyle, Georgina, op.cit., p.44.
14. Doyle, Sir Arthur Conan, op.cit., p.72.
15. Doyle, Georgina, op.cit., p.43.
16. Glaister, John, *A Text-Book of Medical Jurisprudence and Toxicology*, pp.540
17. Stashower, op.cit., p.86.
18. Doyle, Sir Arthur Conan, *Memories and Adventures*, p.90.

19. Television Documentary. *Arthur Conan Doyle: For the Defence*. 2005. Produced and directed by Richard Downes. BBC Scotland. C. BBC.

## Chapter 7: Literary Illusions, Imagery, Music

1. Doyle, Georgina, *Out of the Shadows*. p.246.

## Chapter 9: The Demise of Holmes

1. Stashower, Daniel, *Teller of Tales: The Life of Arthur Conan Doyle*. p.212.
2. Doyle, Sir Arthur Conan, *Memories and Adventures*. p.15.
3. Ibid, p.26.
4. Ibid, p.27.
5. Ibid, p.141.

## Chapter 10: A Quest for Meaning: The Paranormal

1. Gregory, Richard L. (Ed.), *The Oxford Companion to the Mind*. p.577.
2. Ibid, John Beloff, formerly Senior Lecturer, Department of Psychology, University of Edinburgh: 'Parapsychology and the Mind-Body Problem', p.585.
3. Ibid, 'Spiritualistic Research.' p.584.
4. Doyle, Sir Arthur Conan, *Memories and Adventures*. p.77.
5. Matthew, H.C.G. and Harrison, Brian, *Oxford Dictionary of National Biography. Vol.16*, p.828.
6. Doyle, op.cit., p.78.
7. Stashower, Daniel, *Teller of Tales: The Life of Arthur Conan Doyle*. p.98.
8. Doyle, op.cit., p.142.
9. Doyle, Georgina, *Out of the Shadows*. p.111.
10. Doyle, Sir Arthur Conan, *Memories and Adventures*. p.157.
11. Doyle, op.cit., p.195.

## Chapter 11: Holmes is Reborn

1. Doyle, Adrian Conan, *The True Conan Doyle*. pp.10-11.
2. Ibid, p.6.
3. Doyle, Sir Arthur Conan, *The Poems of Arthur Conan Doyle*.
4. Doyle, Adrian Conan. op.cit., p.19.
5. Doyle, Sir Arthur Conan, *Memories and Adventures*. p.215.
6. Doyle, Georgina, *Out of the Shadows*. p.150.

## Chapter 12: Justice and Fair Play

1. Doyle, Sir Arthur Conan, *Memories and Adventures*. p.210.
2. Stashower, Daniel, *Teller of Tales: The Life of Arthur Conan Doyle*. p.257.
3. Ibid, p.258.
4. Doyle, op.cit., p.217.
5. Stashower, op.cit., p.263.
6. Ibid, p.409.

7. Ibid, p.412.
8. *Conan Doyle: For the Defence.* Film documentary produced and directed by Richard Downes. BBC Scotland. 2005.

## Chapter 13: War, Spiritualism

1. Stashower, Daniel, *Teller of Tales: The Life of Arthur Conan Doyle.* p.305.
2. Ibid, p.340.
3  Doyle, Sir Arthur Conan, *Memories and Adventures.* p.343,350,378.
4. Stashower, op.cit., p.324.
5. Ibid, p.52.
6. Ibid, p.335.
7. Ibid, p.334.
8. Ibid, p.334.
9. Doyle, op.cit., pp.392-3.
10. Stashower, op.cit., pp.340-41.
11. Ibid, p.335.
12. Doyle, Adrian Conan, *The True Conan Doyle.* p.17.

## Chapter 14: Fairies

1. Doyle, Adrian Conan, *The True Conan Doyle.* p.10.
2. www.gaeltalk.net/samplelessons/lesson1/culture.php.
3. Doyle, Sir Arthur Conan, *The Coming of the Fairies.* p.13.
4. Ibid, p.17.
5. Ibid, p.29.
6. Ibid, p.53.
7. Ibid, p.111.
8  Cooper, Joe, *The Unexplained.* p.436.
9. Stashower, Daniel, *Teller of Tales: The Life of Arthur Conan Doyle.* pp.361-62.
10. Ibid, p.362.
11. www.unmuseum.org/fairies.htm 29/3/2006. Article by Lee Krystek. 2000.
12. Lamond, Reverend John, *Arthur Conan Doyle: A Memoir.* pp.224-25.
13. Ibid, pp.224-25.

## Chapter 15: Harry Houdini: Further Psychic Experiences

1. Doyle, Sir Arthur Conan, *The Edge of the Unknown*, p.31.
2. Houdini, H., *A Magician among the Spirits.*
3. Stashower, Daniel, *Teller of Tales: The Life of Arthur Conan Doyle*, pp.390-392.
4. Ibid, p.365.
5. Ibid, pp.338,365,442.
6. Ibid, p.369.
7. Ibid, pp.376-77.
8. Ibid, p.358.
9. Doyle, Georgina, *Out of the Shadows*, p.239.
10. Stashower, op.cit., p.366.
11. Doyle, Sir Arthur Conan, *Memories and Adventures*, pp.392-3.

## Chapter 16: The Paranormal: The Present Position

1. Gregory, Richard L. (Ed.), *The Oxford Companion to the Mind*. p.579.
2. Ibid, p.586.
3. Ibid, p.584.
4. Ibid, p.585.
5. Ibid, p.579.
6. Ibid, p.581.
7. Doyle, Georgina, *Out of the Shadows*. pp.239,240-41.
8. Gelder, Michael, Paul Harrison and Philip Cohen, *Shorter Oxford Textbook of Psychiatry*. p.7.
9. Ibid, pp. 10-12.
10. Ibid, p.12.
11. Ibid, p.224.
12. Doyle, Sir Arthur Conan,. *Memories and Adventures*. p.390.
13. Gelder, op.cit., p.212.
14. Ibid, p.7.
15. Ibid, p.269.
16. Ibid, p.10.
17. Ibid, p.10.
18. Ibid, p.312.
19. Gelder, op.cit., p.223.
20. Ibid, p.224.
21. Television Documentary. *Arthur Conan Doyle: For the Defence*. 2005. Produced and directed by Richard Downes. BBC Scotland. C. BBC.

## Chapter 17: Charles Doyle: Like Father, Like Son?

1. Lothian Health Services Archive. LHB7/51/56.
2. Information supplied by Carol Ince, present owner of Blairerno House.
3. Information supplied by Carol Ince of Blairerno.
4. Information supplied by Northern Health Service Archives, A.R.I. Woolmanhill, Aberdeen.
5. Information supplied by Carol Ince of Blairerno.
6. Doyle, Sir Arthur Conan, *Memories and Adventures*. p.4.
7. Ibid, p.11.
8. Dumfries and Galloway Health Board Archives. Letter from Mrs Mary J.E. Doyle to Dr J. Rutherford, 3 December 1892.
9. Glaister, John, *A Text-Book of Medical Jurisprudence and Toxicology*. p.618.
10. Dumfries and Galloway Health Board Archives, op. cit.

## Chapter 18: Charles Revealed Through his Son's Writings?

1. Jones, Kelvin I., *Conan Doyle and the Spirits*. p.32.
2. Stashower, Daniel, *Teller of Tales: The Life of Arthur Conan Doyle*. pp.24-5.
3. Cumbria Record Office, Kendal, Cumbria.
4. 'Medicine – Alcohol-Related Psychosis': Article by Michael Larson, DO. http://www.emedicine.com/MED/topic3113.htm 28/04/2006
5. Lothian Health Services Archive. Transfer Papers LHB7/Unlisted/Jan 1892/14368.

# Chapter 19: Charles Doyle and the Possible Use of Stimulants

1. Gregory, Richard L. (Ed.), *The Oxford Companion to the Mind.* p.570.
2. Ibid, pp.654–54.
3. Gelder, Michael, Paul Harrison, Philip Cohen, *Shorter Oxford Textbook of Psychiatry.* p.465.
4. Journal of Clinical Psychiatry. 1991. Dec; 52(12):509–12.
5. Dumfries and Galloway Health Board Archives. Letter from Mrs Mary J.E. Doyle to Dr J. Rutherford, 3 December 1892.

# Chapter 20: The Montrose Royal Asylum

1. Lothian Health Services Archive. LHB7/51/56.
2. Glaister, John, *A Text-Book of Medical Jurisprudence and Toxicology*, pp.535,540.
3. Lothian Health Services Archive, op.cit., Transfer Papers LHB7/Unlisted/Jan 1892/14368.
4. University of Dundee Archive, Records Management and Museum Services. THB 23/4/1/12.
5. Ibid, THB 23/4/1/14.
6. Ibid, THB 23/4/1/14.
7. Ibid, THB 23/4/1/14.
8. Northern Health Service Archives, ARI Woolmanhill, Aberdeen.
9. Dr Allan Beveridge. Article for the Journal of the Royal Society of Medicine, 2006.
10. University of Dundee Archive, Records Management and Museum Services, op.cit., THB 5/3/7.
11. Ibid, THB 23 5/3/6.

# Chapter 21: Charles Doyle's Diary

1. Doyle, Sir Arthur Conan, *Memories and Adventures.* p.12.
2. Baker, Michael, *The Doyle Diary.* p.81.
3. Gelder, Michael, Paul Harrison, Philip Cohen, *Shorter Oxford Textbook of Psychiatry.* p.7.

# Chapter 22: From Montrose to Edinburgh and Dumfries

1. Lothian Health Services Archive. Transfer Papers LHB7/Unlisted Certification Papers/ Jan.1892/14368.
2. Lothian Health Services Archive. LHB7/51/56.
3. University of Dundee Archive.
4. Dumfries and Galloway Health Board Archives.
5. Catford, E.F., *The Royal Edinburgh Hospital*, pp. 3–5.
6. Gifford, John. Colin McWilliam and David Walker, *Edinburgh. The Buildings of Scotland.* Penguin Books. p.620.
7. Richardson, Harriett. Scottish Hospital Survey.
8. The Scotsman. A Great Doctor. 27 September 1930.
9. Wikipedia, Philippe Pinel. 7/6/2006.
10. The Scotsman, op.cit.
11. Ibid.
12. Lothian Health Services Archive. Case Notes LHB7/51/56.
13. Dumfries and Galloway Health Board Archives.
14. Ibid, letter from Mrs Mary J.E. Doyle to Dr J. Rutherford, 3 December 1892.

15. Baker, Michael, *The Doyle Diary*. p.xvi.
16. Doyle, Georgina, *Out of the Shadows*. p.76.
17. Doyle, Sir Arthur Conan, *Memories and Adventures*. p.4.
18. Ibid, p.25.

# Chapter 23: Charles Doyle: Towards a Diagnosis

1. Gelder, Michael, Paul Harrison, Philip Cohen. *Shorter Oxford Textbook of Psychiatry*. p.331.
2. Ibid, p.335.
3. Epilepsy Action. 'Alcohol and Recreational Drugs.'http://www.epilepsy.org.uk/info/ alcohol.html 28/04/2006.
4. Gelder, op.cit., p.48.
5. Ibid, p.350.
6. Ibid, pp.305,182-83.
7. Ibid, p.442.
8. Ibid, p.457.
9. Dumfries and Galloway Health Board Archives.

# Chapter 24: Doyle's Delusions: An Inherited Disease

1. Engen, Rodney, *Richard Doyle*. P.146.
2. Ibid, pp.145,150.
3. Ibid, p.143.
4. Doyle, Georgina, *Out of the Shadows*. p.225.
5. Ibid, p.248.
6. Ibid, p.249.
7. Gelder, Michael, Paul Harrison, Philip Cohen, *Shorter Oxford Textbook of Psychiatry*. p.281.
8. Gelder, op.cit., p.313.

# Chapter 25: Epilogue

1. Doyle, Adrian Conan, *The True Conan Doyle*. pp.23,18-19.
2. Ibid, p.13.
3. Dumfries and Galloway Health Board Archives. Letter from Mrs Mary J.E. Doyle to Dr J. Rutherford, 3 December 1892.
4. Doyle, Adrian Conan, op. cit., p.18.
5. Lamond, Reverend John, *Arthur Conan Doyle: A Memoir*. p.220.
6. Ibid, p.216.
7. Ibid, p.220.
8. Doyle, Georgina, *Out of the Shadows*. pp.245,252,277.
9. Ibid, p.278.
10. Doyle, Adrian Conan, op. cit., p.14.

# Bibliography

Baker, Michael, *The Doyle Diary*. New York & London: Paddington Press, 1978.
Booth, Martin, *The Doctor, The Detective, and Arthur Conan Doyle*. London: Hodder & Stoughton, 1997.
British Census, 1871, 1881.

Catford, E.F., *The Royal Edinburgh Hospital*. Edinburgh: Scottish Academic Press, 1984.
Cooper, Joe, *The Case of the Cottingley Fairies* (In *The Unexplained*).

Doyle, Adrian Conan, *The True Conan Doyle*. London: John Murray, 1945.
Doyle, Sir Arthur Conan, *The Adventures of Sherlock Holmes*. London: The Reader's Digest Association Ltd, 2001.
Doyle, Sir Arthur Conan, *The Case-Book of Sherlock Holmes*. Ware, Herefordshire, UK: Wordsworth Editions Ltd, 1993.
Doyle, Sir Arthur Conan, *The Coming of the Fairies*. London: Pavilion Books Ltd, 1997.
Doyle, Sir Arthur Conan, *The Edge of the Unknown*. London: John Murray, 1930.
Doyle, Sir Arthur Conan, *His Last Bow*. London: Penguin Books Ltd, 1997.
Doyle, Sir Arthur Conan, *Sherlock Holmes: The Long Stories*. Leicester, UK: Galley Press, 1987.
Doyle, Sir Arthur Conan, *Memories and Adventures*. Boston: Little, Brown and Company, 1924.
Doyle, Sir Arthur Conan, *The Memoirs of Sherlock Holmes*. London: CRW Publishing Ltd, 2005.
Doyle, Sir Arthur Conan, *The Poems of Arthur Conan Doyle*. London: John Murray, 1922.
Doyle, Sir Arthur Conan, *The Return of Sherlock Holmes*. London: The Reader's Digest Association Ltd, 1995.
Doyle, Sir Arthur Conan, *Round the Fire Stories*. USA: Chronicle Books, 1991.
Doyle, Georgina, *Out of the Shadows*. Ashcroft, British Columbia: Calabash Press, 2004.
Doyle, Richard, *Richard Doyle's Journal 1840*. Edinburgh: John Bartholomew & Son, 1980.
Doyle, Richard, *In Fairyland*. London: Michael Joseph, 1870.
Doyle, Richard, *In Fairyland*. Exeter: Paddington Press (UK) Ltd, 1979.
Dumfries and Galloway Health Board Archives.
Dundee, University of: Archive, Records management and Museum services.

Engen, Rodney, *Richard Doyle*. Stroud, Glos. UK: Catalpa Press, 1983.

Gelder, Michael, Paul Harrison, Philip Cowen, *Shorter Oxford Textbook of Psychiatry*. Oxford: Oxford University Press, 2006.

Gifford, John. Colin McWilliam and David Walker, *Edinburgh. The Buildings of Scotland*. London: Penguin Books, 1984.

Glaister, John, *A Text-Book of Medical Jurisprudence and Toxicology*. Edinburgh: E & S Livingstone, 1921.

Gregory, Richard L.,(Ed.), *The Oxford Companion to the Mind*. Oxford University Press, 1987.

Houdini, H., *A Magician among the Spirits*. New York: Harper & Bros, 1924.

Jones, Kelvin I., *Conan Doyle and the Spirits*. Northamptonshire, UK: The Aquarian Press, 1989.

Lamond, Reverend John, *Arthur Conan Doyle: A Memoir*. London: John Murray, 1931.
Lothian Health Service Archives.

Matthew, H.C.G. and Brian Harrison, *Oxford Dictionary of National Biography*. Oxford University Press, 2004.

Norden, Pierre, *Conan Doyle*, London: John Murray, 1966.
Northern Health Service Archives, A.R.I. Woolmanhill, Aberdeen.

Richardson, Harriett, *Scottish Hospital Survey*. (Unpublished. Circa 1980-1990)

Stashower, Daniel, *Teller of Tales: The Life of Arthur Conan Doyle*. London: The Penguin Press, 2000.

Film Documentary:
*Arthur Conan Doyle: For the Defence*. Produced and directed by Richard Downes. BBC Scotland. C. BBC, 2005.

# List of Illustrations

## Black and White Illustrations

## Colour Illustrations

# Index

# Index